CREATED
TO
Live

"Cathy Harris challenges us beyond our own personal healing to seeing with "Kingdom eyes" how we can restore the sanctity of human life by overcoming evil with good. The mission of Jesus' church has never changed—we do justice, we love mercy, and we walk humbly. Cathy has given us a great primer; let's follow her lead."

KAREN A. ELLISON,
President, Deeper Still

"*Created to Live* is a deep and engaging perspective on the effect of abortion on women in the Church and in our nation. This book gives encouragement to praying Christians to carry the torch to end the pain of abortion in our time."

LINDA J. COCHRANE, R.N., CEO,
Author of *Forgiven* and *Set Free*

"Cathy Harris shares stories of pain, grief, hope, and healing with detail, eloquence, and compassion. Those struggling with the pain and sorrow of abortion can find comfort in her words and courage to move forward."

JODY DUFFY,
Director of PATH (Post-Abortion Treatment and
Healing) Atlanta;
Rachel's Vineyard Retreat Site Leader;
Atlanta Regional Coordinator for "Silent No More"

"This book is an amazing collection of truth, wisdom, and love about one of the most important issues of the day. I urge you to read it and be blessed."

ALLAN PARKER,
President, The Justice Foundation & Operation Outcry;
Lead Counsel for Norma McCorvey, "Roe" of Roe v.
Wade and Sandra Cano, "Doe" of Doe v. Bolton

"Cathy is a living testimony of God's grace and redemptive work in the earth. Anyone who has been touched by the horror of abortion will find hope in her story. All who believe that every human child carries the image of God will be inspired by her life's work."

DEAN NELSON,
National Outreach Director, Human Coalition

CREATED TO Live

Becoming the Answer for an
ABORTION-FREE COMMUNITY

Cathy Harris

AMBASSADOR INTERNATIONAL
GREENVILLE, SOUTH CAROLINA & BELFAST, NORTHERN IRELAND

www.ambassador-international.com

Created to Live

Becoming the Answer for an Abortion-Free Community
© 2016 by Cathy Harris
All rights reserved

ISBN: 978-1-62020-571-6
eISBN: 978-1-62020-595-2

Cover Design and Page Layout by Hannah Nichols
eBook Conversion by Anna Riebe Raats

AMBASSADOR INTERNATIONAL
Emerald House
411 University Ridge, Suite B14
Greenville, SC 29601, USA
www.ambassador-international.com

AMBASSADOR BOOKS
The Mount
2 Woodstock Link
Belfast, BT6 8DD, Northern Ireland, UK
www.ambassadormedia.co.uk

The colophon is a trademark of Ambassador

Dedicated to our sweet Hannah
and all the other children who have a name in Heaven.

Contents

FOREWORD

IN 2005, I HAD THE privilege of meeting Cathy Harris at an altar in Washington, D.C., where I shared my personal journey and pain of paying for the abortion of a child I had fathered. That was the first time I had publicly shared my story, and little did I know the ripple effect that would ensue. I also shared and prayed for healing for Cathy and others. After Cathy left the conference for her hometown, she felt led to pray at an abortion clinic in Atlanta, Georgia. She prayed for women and men to change their minds about this life-altering decision, and she prayed for healing for those who would make the same regrettable mistake that would so emotionally damage them. She was also praying for abortion to end in America, and that abortion clinics, like the one in front of her, would close.

As fate would have it, and unbeknownst to her, the clinic Cathy prayed in front of was the same clinic where I had paid for the abortion of the child I had fathered. What are the chances that, of all the clinics she could have chosen to pray in front of, she would find herself in front of the clinic I had gone to some twenty years prior? I don't think it's a coincidence that the clinic, as a result of God answering persistent prayer, closed down on my birthday. Every child who is conceived deserves to have a birthday. God continued using

Cathy's prayers, and later the clinic owner was convicted of Medicaid fraud, was sent to prison, and all of his abortion facilities were closed.

Cathy's story is powerful because it demonstrates the power of our testimony. Truth spoken in love has healing properties that change the world for the better.

I've had the honor of knowing Cathy since 2005, and I can attest that she is one of the most honest, gentle, and yet brave people whom I know. Reading through the pages of this book, I was moved not only by her eloquence, but also by her ability to communicate truth in a manner that compels the reader into the same honesty and transparency that resulted in her healing. The story of her personal journey is going to change your life and will thus have ripple effects that will shape the future for many. This book drips with the love of a merciful God. May this book fuel your personal prayer life and your journey for healing. May the ripple effects of God's love and redemptive power heal the victimized, release justice for the unborn, close more abortion clinics, and result in many more birthday parties.

—Will Ford III

Director, Marketplace Leadership,

Christ for the Nations Institute, Dallas, Texas

Author of *Created for Influence: Transforming Culture From Where You Are*

and *History Makers: Your Prayers Have The Power To Heal The Past and Shape The Future*

If trees were tall and grasses short,
As in some crazy tale,
If here and there a sea were blue
Beyond the breaking pale,

If a fixed fire hung in the air
To warm me one day through,
If deep green hair grew on great hills,
I know what I should do.

In dark I lie; dreaming that there
Are great eyes cold or kind,
And twisted streets and silent doors,
And living men behind.

Let storm clouds come: better an hour,
And leave* to weep and fight,
Than all the ages I have ruled
The empires of the night.

I think that if they gave me leave
Within the world to stand,
I would be good through all the day
I spent in fairyland.

They should not hear a word from me
Of selfishness or scorn;
If only I could find the door;
If only I were born.

—"By the Babe Unborn" (G. K. Chesterton)

*permission

Chapter One

THE DOORWAY

"Here I am! I stand at the door and knock. If anyone hears my
voice and opens the
door, I will come in and eat with that person, and they with me."

Revelation 3:20

ALTHOUGH THEY WERE PLAIN AND uninviting, I saw those double doors as my golden chance to start over. My past would swing shut behind them; my future beckoned me through them. No one on the other side would have to know about my past. No one from the streets of my past would ever barge their way into my present. High school graduation was finally over, and I could run away from it all: the memories, the pain, the boy.

I had no idea where I was running to, but I ran as fast as I could. I was aimless and confused, and those double doors gave me hope. But *could* I walk through them? Could I dare to show my face in a church again? Would they accept me? Would they see through my facade? With these fearful thoughts attempting to hold me back, I pushed through the double doors of the Wesley Foundation, the University of Georgia's United Methodist Student Center. No one could have prepared me for the wonderful future that was awaiting me inside.

My past did also find its way through those doors, however. The boy I had run away from followed me to my university, over 600 miles from our hometown. He found me in my new home, and I was devastated. My two worlds had collided. So I tried to live with one foot in that unsanctified relationship and the other foot in every Christian ministry opportunity available. Bible studies and discipleship meetings filled every moment that I wasn't in class. I was desperate to be the old me again and to leave my past behind. Unfortunately, my past would not let me leave it behind.

I introduced myself to all my new friends as a Methodist minister's daughter, a former youth group leader, and a straight-A Christian college student. That was all I wanted them to know about me—but I knew the real me. I didn't want anyone to learn of my past mistakes—but I could never forget them. The pain from my past and my continuing relationship with my boyfriend haunted all my skillfully planned introductions.

It wasn't until I took my first mission trip, several months later, while surrounded by inner-city kids in Omaha, Nebraska, that I found the courage to leave him. Suddenly, I was seeing children forced to live in terrible situations. I sat with young girls as they talked about their relationships at home and with boys at school. The more I spent time with them on the playground and saw the pain on their faces, the more they reminded me of myself. I was there to be a role model for them, yet my own sin haunted me. I realized that I had a choice to make. I could give myself to the pursuit of holiness and purity, or I could continue in my ungodly romantic relationship. So, steeling my determination and courage, I once again ran from the relationship. But only after moving out of my dorm room for several days, getting a restraining order on my boyfriend, and having my pastor call him was the relationship truly over. Finally, the boy was gone. . . . Yet my secret remained, untouched.

The fall semester began for me at the Wesley Foundation with signs that read, "Welcome to Leadership Training!" With my secret safely hidden in my heart and a smile from ear to ear on my face, I walked through those familiar double doors elated, ready to join the ministry's leadership team. I was excited about this new opportunity, ready to start my life afresh.

That is, until what they called a "confession" packet was placed in my hands. As I stared at the ominous package, the words *confession, purity,* and *sin* leapt off the page at me. My hands began to sweat and my knees shook as I walked to the corner of the room for personal prayer and ministry. I had already ended my four-year-long, impure relationship; was that not enough? I was proud of myself for changing my life. Did I really need to tell anyone about all my other past mistakes? The thought of what could be awaiting me on the pages of the packet caused a lump to form in my throat.

I was paired with someone already on the leadership team; the purpose of the exercise was to confess our past and present unrighteous deeds so we could pray through them and start the year off with a clean slate. It seemed more than a little intrusive to me that we were forced to go through such an exercise; no one *else* had ever asked me to confess my sins. I looked at the person I was paired with, and then glanced back at the double doors. My past had entered through those doors once before; I wasn't sure I could handle another intrusion.

Should I make a run for it? Could I transfer to another student ministry? Could I start all over again? But I was stuck in a room full of people who believed that I was simply a good preacher's kid who happened to have a bad boyfriend in my past. I walked over and sat down.

We began to go through the packet slowly, one page at a time: confessing sins, praying for one another, and sharing our stories. My heart lightened with each turned page. The first few pages were easy. I had never done drugs, never taken a sip of alcohol, never been involved in any kind of occult practice. We even managed to whizz through the page entitled "Sexual Sin." Given the relationship I had just escaped, my prayer partner wasn't surprised to hear my confession. I was even surprised how easily my confession came out. I breathed a sigh of relief and thought my boat was free to sail. My secret was still safe: the word *abortion* was nowhere on the page. I supposed that abortion was so rare that it must not be worth covering in the ministry packet. I would make it out alive after all. Then my friend turned over that sheet of paper and pulled out the next one.

The word *ABORTION* mocked me from the top of the page.

And I began to wail.

I had vowed to always keep my abortion a secret, yet I could not control myself as my emotional pain burst out of my mouth. I bent over, with my head on the floor in front of me, and I wailed. I broke. The floodgates opened, and my emotional vomit spilled out on the floor before the poor girl who was praying with me. I was unable to talk, sit up, or even look anyone in the eye. It felt like everyone in the room was looking at me. How could they not turn their heads and stare at me, stunned that the good little preacher's daughter was actually such a horrible sinner? They knew my secret now. Why else would

I be crying and screaming like a mad woman on the floor, the moment we moved to the section on abortion? Shame covered me like a blanket, yet I felt chills slither down my body instead of warmth.

My terrible secret was out in the open for everyone to see.

> The word ABORTION mocked me from the top of the page.

After a few minutes, my wailing turned to silence, and I found the courage to open my eyes and look up. To my shock, my prayer partner was crying. Other leaders were sitting around me, all with tears in their eyes. Suddenly, all of my expectations were demolished.

My past had barged in again and lain itself out on the floor for everyone to see. My pretty rug was filthy and war-torn. But although my face was red, puffy, and covered in black mascara, my new friends and leaders listened to me and loved me. They chose to invest in me, walk with me, and not disqualify me. Hours and hours of tears, prayer, and counseling followed that day, and I began to build a history with God. God had allowed my past to barge in through those double doors. My two worlds had collided, but to my amazement, the debris of the collision brought forth a beautiful deliverance. I laugh now when I think about my first day of ministry "training" being instead a day of personal deliverance. God knew exactly what I needed, and His infinite wisdom and love led to three years on the leadership team and four more years on staff as the ministry's outreach director. The Wesley Foundation became my home.

My new community was altogether different from the life and relationships I had known before. When I was in high school I had it all together on the outside, but inside, I was broken. Though to my fellow students and teachers I appeared wise beyond my years, my downfall began when I believed a teenage boy when he told me that he loved me. I was the invisible new girl in a high school full of kids who already had friends, and I desperately wanted to belong. This young man saw me, plucked me out of the crowd, and began to pursue me like I had never been pursued before. He waited for me outside of my classes to walk me to the next class. He carried my books and left flowers in my locker. He introduced me to his friends and placed me on a pedestal.

I longed to be known and loved, so I allowed him to. In a fatherless and misguided crowd of teenagers, I became his trophy girlfriend. Slowly, my Christian convictions and values faded into the background, no longer able to get my attention. Before I knew it, though, my boyfriend's loving pursuit turned into four long years of a secretly controlling and sexually abusive relationship. I felt trapped, but no one knew that I needed rescuing.

I woke up one morning, sick to my stomach. After school the next day, a friend walked me to the drug store to buy a home pregnancy test. The package seemed to be burning a hole in my backpack as I walked home. Desperately trying to ignore my new reality, all night long I stared at the ceiling, pretending that there was no home pregnancy test lying there, waiting for me to take it. I knew I was pregnant, but I dreaded to watch as that heartless stick confirmed what I already knew to be true.

The next day I sat in the bathroom, looking at the words I had dreamt of seeing one day in the future, but that terrified me now. I had longed for a loving marriage and the gift of motherhood, yet now I was in the middle of a nightmare. But I pressed my fears deep down inside, wiped the tears from my eyes, loaded on the make-up, and walked out the door to school. My body was moving but my heart stood still, knowing that my life had changed forever.

Thoughts of becoming a parent raced through my mind as I drove to school. But these thoughts were silenced in the school parking lot the moment I told my boyfriend the news. Abortion suddenly rushed into the center of our conversation, silencing any other option. My car seemed to drive itself to the Planned Parenthood clinic, only a mile from our inner-city high school. According to my boyfriend, school could wait for another day. I sat in the lobby of the clinic, trying to convince myself that my baby was not really a baby. I knew deep down that it was my baby, but I needed to hear those deceptive words from my boyfriend, the doctor, and anyone else willing to lie to me before I could go through with the awful decision. I hid behind the lie long enough to make an appointment: on the following Wednesday, during my school study period, I would get an abortion.

Wednesday arrived, and no one had refuted the lie.

The lies I believed before and after my abortion took root and spread throughout my mind like weeds. My abortion became my dirty little secret, a secret I never discussed with anyone, until someone was willing to have a conversation with me about it.

My silence was enabled by my church's silence and the lack of deep, meaningful relationships among the congregation. The only conversations I heard in my high school about teenage pregnancy and abortion came from pro-choice media, friends, and Planned Parenthood themselves. Because my church never discussed the issue, I assumed that I was the only Christian in my town who had ever been involved in an abortion; I thought that I was one of the few Christians alive who had ever committed such a serious sin. Little did

I know that I was part of an epidemic sweeping the nation. I wonder now how many other women were sitting there with me in those same church pews hiding the same secret? What would have happened if someone had dared to discuss the issue?

A simple conversation and a moment of loving accountability was all it took to unlock my caged spirit. One bold conversation was all it took to set me on a path to a new life. Once my secret was out, the basic Christian life was no longer basic—being a Christian suddenly became nothing like I had known before. My soul was set free, and became a sponge for new and refreshing teachings on the Holy Spirit; God's amazing, boundless love; and the Christian disciplines of fasting, prayer, and giving. I devoted myself to the scriptures and to accountability with God and other believers, and God set me on a fast-paced journey into His heart.

I soon began sharing my story as a counselor in a pregnancy center; I joined the advisory board for an adoption agency; and I also shared my story at the Wesley Foundation to hundreds of students, hoping that I could be the one to begin the abortion conversation for other girls like me. It was an honor to allow God to use my story to save another girl or baby. It was deeply refreshing to be able to finally move on from my abortion decision. At least I thought I could move on.

It was 2005 when my best friend and I decided to take a spontaneous road trip to Washington, D.C. We had heard stirrings of a worship and prayer gathering taking place there that we desperately wanted to attend. Having no money, no place to stay, and no exact address for the gathering, we headed off on an adventure, to see what God was up to. After roaming the streets of D.C., finding a building shaped like an arrow (this was the only information we had on the location), and jumping in a van with total strangers who said they were associated with the gathering, we finally ended up at a church. We walked into a room full of hundreds of other believers. The atmosphere was electric, and I immediately felt a connection with everyone else in the room, even though my friend was the only person there whom I had known for more than a few minutes. It was strange how at home I felt. I somehow sensed that a holy moment was just around the corner.

After several hours of losing ourselves in the worship of God, a hush came over the room as the leader of the gathering, Lou Engle, began to speak. The moment he opened his mouth, my hands began to sweat and tears began flowing down my cheeks. The conviction of the Lord, but also His kindness, flowed over me as Lou announced that the primary prayer topics for the night were revival . . . and the ending of abortion in America.

Working in a pregnancy center as I did, I was constantly around people who spoke about abortion, yet I had never heard anyone speak with such clarity and such conviction on the issue—and certainly never from a pulpit.

Lou's words cut me deeply. Once again I found myself face down on the floor, completely undone. As Lou spoke, I realized that I had still not come face to face with the reality of what I had done. I squinted at the truth, knowing that a full gaze would be bitter. But the words coming from this man cut through the bone and marrow of my mental defenses. They were sharper than a double-edged sword, cutting through the fatty excess of my illusions and denial.

For the first time since my abortion, I listened to a pastor boldly tell me the unvarnished truth about my decision. Up until then, no one had been brutally honest with me. Of course I knew that my decision to abort my child had been wrong, but until Lou spoke, I could not accept that I had actually killed my child. I listened as Lou and others spoke on the history of abortion, abortion statistics in America, and the truth about the abortion industry. At times my stomach hurt so bad I thought I was going to vomit. The stories I heard from women, former abortion clinic workers, and Norma McCorvey, "Jane Roe" of *Roe v. Wade*, wrecked me emotionally. I realized that I had bought into a lie much bigger than myself. My baby had become a statistic, one of millions of innocent children murdered for greed by doctors and business people.

The pain of remembering my abortion decision turned to mourning, and then to deep intercession for our nation. Then I felt that God was calling my name from the front of the room. He plucked me out of the crowd, reminded me of His forgiveness, and commissioned me. Somehow I found myself on the stage of the prayer meeting, sharing my story with a room full of strangers. My healing journey had suddenly become about more than me and my own experiences: I knew that God was calling me to a life of intercession, and to be a voice for the unborn and for women in America. I had no idea what that looked like or where to go from there, but my heart said yes to His plans.

As I left the prayer meeting, I felt that a new authority was on my voice. I knew I had gone somewhere new with God in my healing journey. When I arrived back home, I found that my testimony had taken on a life of its own. Invitations to speak were suddenly coming from every direction. To my amazement, I found myself sharing my story in congressional hearings, abortion recovery meetings, on the steps of my state capitol, the steps of the United States Supreme Court building, and a few years later at The Call Nashville, a national prayer gathering, in a stadium of over 70,000 people.

I was humbled, and trying to be faithful with the ministry God had suddenly given me. As exciting as it was to minister with God and see women all across the nation set free from the pain of abortion, my heart was also broken as I realized just how many women were suffering in silence. With every opportunity to speak came an opportunity to pray. My heart was alive in God, but I mourned over the state of our nation. I desperately desired a greater intimacy with Jesus and to know His heart better. So I decided that it was time to take a leap of faith, and I left the college ministry and the pregnancy center where I had spent the last seven years of my life, and began interning at the Atlanta International House of Prayer (IHOP). My six-month internship was devoted to learning the discipline of prayer and intercession. My primary role was being an intercessory missionary, which meant that I sat in a room for hours with other believers as we prayed for Atlanta, the nation, world events, and other topics God was highlighting, just as Anna and Simon remained in the temple praying until Jesus came to Earth.

Although I was usually tucked away in the IHOP prayer room, God still called me out several times to return to Washington, D.C., for prayer gatherings. I was also asked to lead Bound4Life Atlanta, a pro-life outreach and prayer ministry under the guidance of IHOP. God used that opportunity to teach me persistence in prayer and faith to believe for the impossible. We partnered in prayer with several key governmental players in Atlanta working on pro-life legislation, and traveled to churches where we spoke about the cruel realities behind abortion. God gave our leadership team the audacious faith to believe that He could end abortion in our city, one abortion clinic at a time. So we decided to start taking a consistent stand in front of one of the most successful abortion clinics in Atlanta, praying that God would close it, and also completely end abortion in our city. We knew that if we kept showing up, God would eventually shut it down.

We dedicated ourselves to a consistent stand on the sidewalk across the street from the abortion clinic. We prayed silently, took communion, and built relationships with the pro-choice women yelling at us from in front it. The sidewalk quickly became our intercessory battleground. We stood in the heat, the snow, and the rain, believing God for a miracle. We knew that with God, anything is possible. We wept as we saw teenagers walk into the clinic holding their mother's hand. We wept as we witnessed women with large bellies go through the doors with determined steps . . . and leave with a look of death on their faces. We were determined that this would end. Then, one day, it did. Just like that, a "Closed" sign was posted on the front door of the clinic, and a notice was posted on their website. Finally, it was over. Later we discovered that the abortionist had been arrested and put in prison for Medicaid fraud. God had uncovered his bloodshed and ungodly deeds, and He had allowed us to partner with Him. As I stood and stared at the now-locked door to the clinic, I cried tears of both sadness and relief, and my faith in God soared.

With the closing of the clinic, I felt released from Atlanta to continue my pilgrimage to Washington, D.C. The decisions happening inside the governmental buildings, the stories unfolding in the row homes filing the streets, and the mysteries of what was yet to come on the political stage all beckoned me to be a part of their unfolding. This historic city had found a place in my heart the day I had wandered around it, trying to find where God was gathering people to pray. I had been clueless, but God had been directing my steps on a much greater journey than I could have imagined. So I came back to the building shaped like an arrow, which was the Justice House of Prayer. With my faith greatly increased by my ministry experiences, by sharing my testimony with Congressmen and crowds, and by the closing of the clinic in Atlanta, I joined the JHOP staff. I had faith that God could end abortion in America and, for no other reason than that He is kind, He wanted me to be a part of His wonderful purposes for America. I spent a year on staff with JHOP, leading their morning prayer room sessions and joining their daily stand at the bottom of the steps of the Supreme Court, praying for the ending of abortion in America. My faith was building for revival in America.

God had also brought my personal life full circle. Two years earlier, while on stage at a prayer gathering, God had introduced me to the man of my dreams: my husband, Marcus. Suddenly, I found myself living a life I would never have dreamed possible just a few years before. I was no longer a fearful teenager running from life, but I had now fully embraced who I was in God: a woman fighting for the life of unborn children, and with a new baby in my own womb.

The birth of my baby brought me into a new season: motherhood. I decided to leave the Justice House of Prayer and take care of the little life I had been given. In many ways, I left behind everything but my family. Although I had been fighting for the lives of women and unborn children across our country, I knew now that it was time to protect my own. I stepped out of the whirlwind and into the nursery. My days suddenly became far from glamorous and exciting. The stages were gone, the lights were turned down, and there I was with my beautiful baby. I was thankful for the quiet moments. I took in the smell of my new baby as I reflected on the previous few years.

Chapter Two

THE GOOD, THE BAD, AND THE SHOCKING

You may choose to look the other way,

but you can never say again that you did not know.

William Wilberforce

UNLIKE MANY OTHER WOMEN, MY abortion decision was not made in the midst of extreme poverty or crisis. Although my abortion story did begin in an inner-city high school, I was also involved in a church youth group and was raised in a Christian family. In fact, my father was a pastor. So although giving birth to my child would have been difficult for me, it would have been more than possible. But I was blind to that truth, as are so many thousands of women and teenage girls in America today.

Political debates, shameful stigmas, preserved reputations, and business cash cows all work to divert our attention away from the reality of abortion in our society. Many people's hearts have grown numb, despite a baby being killed every 26 seconds in

America. Abortion has gone from the stated intent of being "safe, legal, and rare" to becoming one of the leading causes of death in our nation. Millions of women, men, and families have been left devastated by abortion. Abortion has wiped out a significant portion of an entire generation.

National Right to Life reports that, from 1973 to 2008 and in the United States alone, almost 58,000,000 (fifty-eight million) abortions have been performed.[1] It is horrifying to contemplate all those children killed; this should cause us all to bow our heads, get on our knees, pray for mercy, and be ready to be the solution. Thankfully, the numbers of abortions in the United States per year are declining.[2] There has also been a significant increase in pro-life legislation, a decrease in the number of abortion clinics, and an increase in the number of pregnancy centers and adoption agencies. Miraculously, we are also seeing abortion doctors and workers leaving the industry, as well as an increasing number of women sharing their abortion stories. These are huge victories, but millions of women, men, and babies are still in the midst of the battle, hoping to be rescued.

> Abortion has gone from the stated intent of being "safe, legal, and rare" to becoming one of the leading causes of death in our nation.

As a nation, we have largely focused on the woman's "right to choose," and we have lost sight of the devastation in our own backyards. In recent days, pictures, videos, and testimonials have blasted nationwide the

---

1   *The State of Abortion in the United States* (Washington D.C.: National Right to Life Committee, 2016), p. 5, http://www.nrlc.org/uploads/communications/stateofabortion2016.pdf.

2   Ibid.

ungodly and abominable acts taking place on all sides of abortion in our nation. I have been in courtrooms, retreats, pregnancy centers, and living rooms and heard with my own ears horrific stories that many women and men have walked through. How can such things be occurring in America? Logic and common sense have been deserted. Apathy and indifference continue to sweep through our church halls. How can it be that we can hear these stories and not be moved? It is easier to cover our eyes and wish that it were all a horrible nightmare.

But if we intend to partner with God and live out our destiny as the Church today, we must open our eyes and walk in the light. Contrary to what the mainstream media tells us, I believe that ours is the pro-life generation. We have had powerful pro-choice voices in previous generations, but coming to the forefront is a new breed of believers who are relentlessly dedicated to seeing truth prevail. The choice is ours. The days of hanging in the balance are over. The grey area is quickly becoming black or white.

Abortion is the taking of the life of an innocent human being, and hundreds of thousands of babies are aborted in America every year. No matter how hard we might wish otherwise, the epidemic of abortion is real. Regardless of the difficult circumstances surrounding a pregnancy, it is simply not possible to end an innocent life in a more godless way than deliberate killing. Whether it's done for our own selfish gain, financial success, or an attempt to escape the consequences of sin doesn't change that fact. A human life is either worthy to be lived or it is not. There is no center of the aisle on this issue.

On January 22, 1973, two landmark cases together opened the door to abortion on demand through all three trimesters of pregnancy for any reason in America. We know these cases as Roe v. Wade and Doe v. Bolton. Many people are not as familiar with Doe v. Bolton, which took Roe v. Wade a step further, allowing late-term abortions and abortions for any reason: abortions past the baby's point of viability. In both cases, the court determined that the word "person" in the 14th Amendment of the United States Constitution did not include unborn children. This interpretation means that the preborn child does not have a Constitutional right to life. Although Justice Blackmun, who authored the court's opinion, stated that if "personhood is established, the appellant's case, of course, collapses, for the fetus's right to life would then be guaranteed specifically by the Amendment (14th)."[3] The question of personhood was at the forefront in these landmark cases, and it continues to be at the forefront of all cases that have followed.

So the question is, have we, in the last 40 years, established what *personhood* is? I propose that we have. Many cases have continued to go before the Court to make a dent in the shaping and devastating actions that have followed these two landmark cases. We have experienced victories as well as disappointments. Yet, regardless of what the courts have decided or will ever decide, we, the Church, cannot allow man's decisions to dictate our actions and opinions. Even in the path of the harshest winds, God's Word stands forever, and it is His Word that we must live by.

These 1973 abortion cases were a devastating pro-choice advancement for our nation. Although devastating, the cases were

---

3   *Roe v. Wade*, The Supreme Court of the United States, 410 U.S. 113, 1973.

not spontaneous. The stage was strategically set. An ideology once openly defined as *Eugenics* became masked as "encouraged steriliza-tions and birth control." With the help of one of its most influential leaders, Margaret Sanger, the birth control movement ushered us into the establishment of what we know today as Planned Parenthood Federation of America.

Webster's dictionary defines *eugenics* as "a science that tries to im-prove the human race by controlling which people become parents." The eugenics movement in America began in the 1800s, gained steam during the early 1900s, and began to take deep root in our soil after World War II. The eugenics movement has been funded by some of our wealthiest citizens and strongly supported by many in academia.[4] The explicit goal of this growing movement was to weed out "feeble-minded"[5] and—note this chilling phrase—"genetically inferior races."[6] After World War II, eugenicists locked arms with birth control advo-cates and the loud voices of the feminist movement, who were after the same goal: population control.

Steering the birth control movement were political radicals such as Margaret Sanger, a eugenicist herself. Partnering with its eugenicist beliefs, the birth control movement targeted minority neighborhoods in order to eliminate the "undesirables," as Margaret called them.[7] Margaret Sanger's "Negro Project," which began in 1939, was created specifically to eliminate African-Americans who were uneducated and so were believed to be a burden on the rest of

---

4   George Grant, *Grand Illusions: The Legacy of Planned Parenthood*, 2nd ed. (Franklin, TN: 1992), 61.

5   Margaret Sanger, "The Eugenic Value of Birth Control Propaganda," *Birth Control Review*, 1921, p. 5.

6   Margaret Sanger, *The Pivot of Civilization* (New York, 1922), 264.

7   Green, Tanya L., "The Negro Project: Margaret Sanger's Eugenic Plan for Black Americans," Concerned Women for America, 1 May 2001.

the population.[8] Unfortunately, many African-American ministers got swept up into this deception. In a letter which Margaret Sanger wrote to a friend, Dr. Clarence Gamble, she said, "We do not want word to go out that we want to exterminate the Negro population, and the minister is the man who can straighten out the idea if it ever occurs to any of their more rebellious members."[9] This project was only the beginning of the devastation caused by abortion in our nation, not only in the African-American community but now in every community.

Planned Parenthood Federation of America, the largest abortion provider in our nation, was founded out of the birth control movement. Initially primarily providers of birth control, slowly these clinics took on abortion as their primary service, as the neighborhoods and nation at large became more accepting of the procedure. The fight to make abortion legal began as these demonic and deceptive values took root in our soil. This was the birth of Planned Parenthood as we know it today. From its conception to its maturity, the same values—deceit, lies, and the deliberate, cold-blooded extermination of innocent human beings—underlie this organization. Margaret Sanger's goals and successes—which, we mustn't forget, were to eliminate anyone deemed "socially inadequate"—are praised throughout the pro-choice movement. Eugenicist beliefs have steamrolled through our nation, and as a result, abortion is now a household reality.

Even the steps that took abortion through the 6-ton bronze doors of the Supreme Court were soaked in the mud of deceit. *Roe v. Wade*, a

---

8   Ibid.
9   Margaret Sanger's December 19, 1939 letter to Dr. Clarence Gamble of Massachusetts, as quoted in Linda Gordon, *Woman's Body, Woman's Right: A Social History of Birth Control in America* (New York: Grossman, 1976).

legal tornado out of Texas, and *Doe v. Bolton*, a tornado out of Georgia, both found their traction through two women, Norma McCorvey (Roe) and Sandra Cano (Doe). Both of these women have repeatedly said that they were manipulated and taken advantage of by their lawyers in order to push an ideological agenda. Neither of them understood the intent nor the impact that their cases would have. Sandra Cano has publicly stated that she turned to a lawyer simply to get her children back from foster care. Her lawyer deviously and without Sandra's knowledge capitalized on her situation to advance the lawyer's own political agenda. Sandra learned that her case had reached the Supreme Court not from her attorney, but while watching the evening news on television in her living room. Sandra, pregnant at the time, never wanted to have an abortion and never had one, even after her case was won.

Norma McCorvey was pregnant and afraid and also turned to her lawyer, Sarah Weddington, for help. Although her request to have an abortion was also used to further a national agenda, Norma never received the help she sought. Like Sandra, she was completely unaware of what the lawyer was actually using her case for. She was simply a poor, uneducated, and scared woman who asked someone for help. Her pro-choice lawyer and others promised to help her yet, according to Norma, from the moment her case won in the Supreme Court they ostracized her, purposely excluded her from events celebrating the *Roe v. Wade* decision, and now desperately try to cover up her story. "In general, the pro-abortion crowd resented the fact that Norma McCorvey was historically tied to legalized abortion."[10] She was a "blue-collar,

---

10   Norma McCorvey, *Won by Love* (Nashville, TN: Thomas Nelson:, 1997), 45.

rough-talking embarrassment."[11] She was merely a means to their end.

Both women are now Christians, pro-life, and have fought to overturn their famous court cases. Norma has worked to expose the insurmountable number of lies that her case was based upon, such as the lie that she was raped. Sandra Cano was a dear personal friend of mine; I met her during my time in ministry in Atlanta. We partnered and prayed together often. Sadly, she passed away recently due to cancer, but for years she shared and wept over the tragedy forever attached to her name. Tragically, and despicably, Norma and Sandra were callously used to advance one of the most horrific agendas of death and deception our country has ever experienced. Both women have suffered greatly as a result.

I have been told that times have changed, that the ideals that shaped the pro-choice movement in the past are no longer what fuel it. I understand that times have changed, but we can easily see that the underlying ideals of the pro-choice movement have not changed since Margaret Sanger's days. Seventy-eight percent of Planned Parenthood clinics are still in minority communities, and for every one black child born, three are aborted.[12] In addition, 90% of unborn babies diagnosed with Down's syndrome are aborted.[13] And despite the primary targets of this tornado, the death of an innocent is still the underlying goal. History has repeated itself. Just as in the days of slavery in our nation, we are

---

11   Ibid., 21.
12   Grant, *Grand Illusions,* 99.
13   Caroline Mansfield, et al. "Termination Rates After Prenatal Diagnosis of Down Syndrome, Spina Bifida, Anencephaly, and Turner and Klinefelter Syndromes: A Systematic Literature Review," Psychology and Genetics Research Group. London, UK. March 1999.

in effect still debating whether every human being truly deserves the Constitutionally-guaranteed right to life. Although personally I believe that many (and perhaps even most) pro-choice individuals and abortion workers genuinely desire to help women, their intentions do not change the reality of their actions. Regardless of our intentions, whether we are setting appointments at the desk of a Planned Parenthood clinic or a Christian believer with our head in the sand, we are still partnering with death.

This blunt fact can be difficult to accept when our heart strings are tugged by the horrific situations some women—and even young girls!—find themselves in. The abortion debate often comes to a screeching halt when someone brings up the life of the mother or the cases of rape and incest. These situations are tragic, yet they are also extremely rare, so we cannot allow them to dictate our opinion of all other abortions. These are extremely difficult situations that should certainly bring us to our knees in prayer and compassion. But we mustn't allow compassion for one person to blind us to the whole truth; we mustn't allow ourselves to condone sin or to have no compassion for other people who are also affected. Jesus did not condemn sinners, yet He also never condoned their sin. He exposed sin in love and kindness. Thankfully, the truth of what is taking place inside abortion clinics continues to be exposed. Yet the question remains: Have our eyes really been opened? Have we moved beyond simply having compassion to seeing the full truth? I propose to you that we can have both.

At what point did we begin believing that having a baby meant the end of a woman's life, of her hopes, dreams, and future success? In my dramatic 17-year-old mind, I equated having a baby to dying.

Seriously. Yes, it is true that achieving some of my dreams and reaching my goals, such as graduating from high school and college, would have been more difficult—but certainly not impossible. I know many women who have done it. I know women who are doing it now. Having a baby is not the end of the mother's life; yet many women need practical and emotional assistance to be able to walk the road to birth and caring for their child.

The stories surrounding abortion decisions are far more complicated than a simple, "do not do it because it is a sin." Too often, in the middle of the fight for pro-life legislations and well-intended efforts to end abortions, many times we have not communicated our love and compassion for the mothers. If we had, would Christian women still be getting abortions at the rates that they are? Furthermore, would those who have had abortions be sitting in silence for ten to fifty years in our church pews? We are going in the right direction, but we need to do so much more.

We need to ask ourselves: Why are women in our communities and churches choosing abortion? The difficult reasons, such as rape and incest, are of course exceptionally hard, yet they represent less than 1% of all abortions.[14] Women are largely choosing abortion for other reasons, such as being too young, not wanting to be connected with the man for the rest of their life, future plans and dreams, finances, unexpected pregnancy out of wedlock, finished with having children, etc. This was me. I was seventeen years old and in a relationship with a boy who I was already trying to leave. The last thing I wanted to do was have a child with him. I also

---

14   National Abortion Federation, "Women Who Have Abortions," Washington D.C., 2003, prochoice.org/education-and-advocacy/about-abortion/abortion-facts/.

wanted to go to college and be a kid myself a little longer. These reasons sounded perfectly legitimate to me at the time; yet all of my perfectly understandable reasons had one very important thing in common. They all began with "I." I wanted a better future. I wanted to go to college. I wanted to escape my relationship. It was all about me.

In the midst of my fear and shame, I made a life-and-death decision. I needed someone to help me see past myself. I needed someone to tell me that I could have my baby. But my overwhelming emotions controlled my heart and my mind. This is normal when we experience trauma, shock, and unexpected circumstances. It can be very difficult to see clearly without the insight of someone else. I wasn't looking ten, fifteen, and twenty years down the road. I was only seventeen years old, and all I saw was my immediate circle of high school friends. Christians need to step into these hard situations and help. Sometimes we must be willing to step inside the high school circle of reputations and dreams. We have to step inside the college-girl circle of career and ambition, or even the circle of rape and trauma. We have to step inside her shoes and understand the complexity of her situation.

The problem is that many women who are having abortions, especially those in the church, like me, are not giving their community, parents, or pastors the opportunity to help. Why do you think that is? For years, women have heard that abortion is a sin. Women have witnessed the great battle of trying to defund Planned Parenthood, pass pro-life legislation, and other great and necessary pro-life efforts to end and limit abortions. If all a woman has heard from her pastor and leaders is about their great pro-life efforts and the tragedy of abortion in our nation, what does she do when she finds herself in the middle of the battle, broken and bruised? Where does a single woman in the church turn when she finds herself in an unexpected pregnancy? Her birth control has failed her, her sexually active relationship has failed her, and now where does she go? She sees the church with closed arms, yet sees Planned Parenthood's doors swinging wide open. She may know intellectually that abortion is wrong, but she desperately needs practical help, and fast.

A recent survey was sponsored by Care Net, a network of pregnancy centers. Over 1,000 women who had abortions were asked about their church attendance and what led them to their abortion decisions. The survey found that "a whopping 70% of women who consider an abortion consider themselves a Christian."[15] In fact, 65% of those women felt that the personal shame and the judgmental nature of their church contributed to their decision to choose an abortion as a quiet and hidden way to end their pregnancy."[16] Only 9% of the women believed that their church was informed about pregnancy options. Only 14% believed that their church community would be helpful if asked for support.[17]

In light of these tragic numbers, a recent article posted by Intercessors for America, "How the Church Can Defund Planned Parenthood without Legislation," proposed a cutting question: "Are we, the Church, to blame for the attraction of abortion to many who are unwed and pregnant?"[18] Of course we can't completely

---

15   "Study of Women Who Have Had an Abortion and Their Views on Church," Lifeway Research, Nov. 2015, p. 32.

16   Ibid., 6.

17   Ibid.

18   Timothy C. Morgan, "How the Church Can Defund Planned Parenthood

blame ourselves for the choices of others, but this is a vital question. Have we created a culture of shame and judgment in our churches that not only requires perfection, but that makes our church fellowships an uncomfortable place for sinners? Sinners were certainly exhorted by Jesus to change their lives, but they also flocked to be in His presence. Can we say the same for our churches in America today?

Scott McConnell, the Vice President of Lifeway Research, believes that the survey results "point to a church culture that often lacks grace."[19] He adds that these results present "a huge opportunity for the church to have an impact on those decisions."[20] These statistics are hard to swallow, yet they are eye-opening. They clearly reveal that we must change our approach; or else we need some divine winds to blow on those approaches that are working. We must continue in our legislative battles and bold efforts to expose deception, but many of these bold approaches are merely an effort to close the door to abortion to those in our own communities.

What if our church communities became "abortion-free communities?" What if we could persuade Christians to stop walking through the doors of Planned Parenthood and instead start showing up on the doorsteps of ministry leaders, youth pastors, and trusted friends? What would happen to the abortion industry if Christians stopped using its services? This is how we need to end abortion in America.

Without Legislation," Intercessors for America, Dec. 2015, www.getamericapraying.com/blog/how-the-church-can-defund-planned-parenthood-without-legislation/.

19   Lisa Cannon Green, "Women Distrust Church on Abortion," Lifeway Research, Nov. 2015, lifewayresearch.com/2015/11/23/women-distrust-church-on-abortion/.

20   Ibid.

I will always remember one of the sweetest clients I worked with at my local pregnancy center. She walked in our door with her hands shaking as she asked for a pregnancy test. Before giving her the test, I decided to spend some time with her in one of our counseling rooms. I knew that if she heard that she actually was pregnant in the midst of her terror, she would not be able to handle it. Her situation was much like mine had been. She was only seventeen, and with a boy who she believed did not even like her. She hoped she would graduate from college and get a good job, and she was a Christian. After spending some time getting to know her, I gave her the test, and we waited, holding hands, as we looked at the test results appear. Slowly the word 'Pregnant' appeared, and she melted into my arms. Together, we sat on the floor of the testing room and wept.

I thought about what I had needed to hear, years before, when I was in her situation. I lifted her chin, smiled at her, and said "Congratulations, Momma." She looked at me, confused, and then she smiled. Truth swept into the room and melted her heart, and we were soon listening to the heartbeat of her sweet baby. After that day, I saw my new friend every week throughout her pregnancy. We talked about her plans. We learned about parenting. We researched adoption options. We met with her mother together. We prayed, and prayed some more. I helped her come up with a plan for schooling and prenatal care. We walked the road together. There were many tears, but there were many more smiles. She was still scared, but she was not alone.

I had the pleasure of holding her baby girl many times after she was born, and for several years she texted me pictures on her baby's birthday. I will never forget the text I received when her daughter turned five years old. It read, "This is my baby girl, Cathy. She is five years old now. Thank you for being our angel."

I was overwhelmed. Had my small efforts truly made such a huge difference in her life? I was already volunteer-

> Offering to hold someone's hand is sometimes all it takes to save their life.

ing at the pregnancy center every Friday, so it had been easy to set aside an extra hour for her each week. In most of our meetings I did not have wise words, or any words at all, but my presence and my consistency made the difference. I didn't condemn this woman when I met with her, but I did tell her truth. In moments of intense emotion and fear, she needed a friend to tell her the truth, not just what she wanted to hear. She needed truth spoken in love and with a hand reached out, ready to take the journey with her. It was an honor for my hand to be that hand. Her life and her baby's life were worth it.

One in four women in our nation will have an abortion by the time they are thirty.[21] Even if you never hear about it, it is likely that someone you know has had an abortion, or will have one. Abortion is an epidemic that is ravaging our generation. Even more tragic, this epidemic is virtually unnoticed. Women who have had abortions are all around us. They are in the pew sitting next to us. They are in the grocery store line behind us. They might be one of your friends, your sister, your mother, . . . and possibly even your wife.

---

21   "Induced Abortion in the United States," Guttmacher Institute, New York, May 2016, p. 1.

In all my years of counseling expectant mothers, I have rarely had a woman walk out still wanting to have an abortion after hearing the truth, hearing her baby's heartbeat, and knowing that we would support her.

It is humbling to realize that all we have to do, sometimes, to save another person's life—is simply offer to hold their hand.

Chapter Three

CREATING A CULTURE OF LIFE

When it comes to life, the critical thing is

whether you take things for granted or take them with gratitude.

—G. K. Chesterton

ARE YOU PRO-LIFE? THIS MIGHT be a more complex question than perhaps you've thought it to be. We might feel compelled to choose one side of the aisle or the other. We may join one interest group over another. Though it is important, even voting for a pro-life candidate behind a curtain at the polls is not going to change our culture on its own. We have to take a bolder stance. Being pro-life is a way of life. It is pro-child, pro-woman, and pro-family. It is pro-people. It startles me that we would consider any other stance. I am pro-life because I love God and I love people. I am pro-life because I realize that my life is not more valuable than another's.

We cannot always choose the easy road. It is easy to say that we are pro-life and give a look of disappointment towards someone who is not. It is easy to vote for a pro-life political candidate behind a curtain. It might even be easy for us to give to an organization that is fighting for pro-life legislation or providing pregnancy tests to women in crisis pregnancies. These are all good efforts, and I'm a proponent of them, but do they impact our lives? I have found that my heart remains distant if I consistently take the easy road.

I liken this to the principles of tithing and giving in Scripture. Tithing is simply giving back to God what is already His. It is not a sacrifice; it is a commandment. But giving an offering beyond the tithe often requires sacrifice. We give because our hearts compel us to give, and we are blessed in the process. Being pro-life is a way of life that may require giving of ourselves, our resources, and our time. Without putting love into action, our words are nothing more than a "noisy gong or a clanging cymbal" (1 Corinthians 13:1–3). With any social issue, if we do not *love people* while we share the truth of the gospel, what are we doing?

> It is time for us to allow God to interrupt our lives.

I have a dream to see abortion-free communities. I am believing for entire church communities to experience the miracle of being abortion-free. This is a bold prayer, but I believe that it is possible. I believe that if churches and communities throughout our nation will operate as pro-life communities, take up abortion in prayer, and transform their own community, we will see abortion numbers decrease dramatically. Our pro-life churches will become who they say there are. A church that is pro-life experiences life within its walls. God will always bless us with children, in planned as well as unplanned circumstances; when a community chooses to receive all of God's blessings, it becomes an abortion-free community.

It is time for us to allow God to interrupt our lives. It is time for us to put our money and our time where our mouth is. The years of merely talking about being pro-life are over. We all have to do what it takes to build up healthy people in our communities, disciple them, love and honor them, lead them well, and support them in the ways in which people need to be supported. We need safe places where people can be real and are allowed to make mistakes. Everyone has seen horrific abortion videos and pictures, and they have heard the great debates. Now, someone needs you to hold their hand. It is time to put our love into action. And our action begins with transforming our own communities.

One of the most powerful ways by which we can transform our communities is by creating a culture within our own church body that protects, nurtures, and shepherds lives well. God may want to partner with you or your church in big ways, such as starting a pregnancy center or an adoption agency in your church. You might be called to many seemingly small (yet actually huge) efforts, such as providing an abortion recovery Bible study, discussing abortion in a sermon series, walking alongside a woman and her pre-born child . . . or simply holding someone's hand. There are many practical ways that we can all help, but creating a culture that promotes life in our church and community lays a foundation of truth on which we can then build any specific practical effort we feel called to. It will also help to sustain the effort of people and families giving their strengths and talents.

According to Webster's dictionary, a culture is "a way of thinking, behaving, or working that exists in a place or organization." The culture of a church community is comprised of the topics of our conversations, sermons, and small groups. It is made up of our core values, the direction and vision we have for the church, and how we spend our time. Creating, or changing, the culture of a community takes time and effort. It requires intentionality from all parties, especially the leadership.

Although we all may have different ways by which we build culture in our communities, churches, and organizations, I have found that building a culture always begins with a conversation. To build a culture of life, we have to be willing to initiate a conversation about abortion, adoption, and even God's value for all life. The culture is then built upon a series of continual conversations. All of us naturally talk about the things that are important to us. When we continually create conversations around those values, passion exudes from us to others that join in on the conversation. When the conversation is brought to the forefront of the community by its leaders, it has the power, over time, to shift the entire community.

I liken this concept to the culture that my husband and I desire to create in our home. If we are continually talking about our love for the Lord and each other around our children, the culture of our home will exude love for God and one another. When we teach and demonstrate faithfulness, peace, and gratitude, these things make up the culture of our family. Our children naturally take hold of the things we place value on through our time, our conversation, and our passions. As parents, we lead our children into the spaces we create.

On the other hand, merely hinting at something, or simply mentioning it once in a while, does not bring about the same results. In addition, if we are completely silent on a topic, we can't expect our community or flock to naturally embrace it. We have to be intentional if we truly desire a value to become one of our core values. Being intentional becomes easier as our passion and understanding of the topic grows, and as we are willing to be vulnerable and transparent with one another along the way. We all naturally talk about the things that are of value to us; those things become a part of the thread that weaves us all together. But we have to create space for those conversations to happen and into which people can dive deep. Soon even a topic such as abortion, that was once an uncomfortable topic of conversation, will become normal.

When we create a culture of life, we show that we value one another. Therefore, our initiated conversations transform into an investment in one another, as well as space for true connection, accountability, and vulnerability to take place.

MARRIAGE & FAMILY

When creating a culture of life, it is necessary that we begin with our most intimate relationships before believing that we can transform any other community that we are a part of. We should first ask ourselves, does my family and marriage value life? Do we value one another, and do we create conversations about each other's value? Investing in our families and marriages is our first ministry, and when we create a culture of life among ourselves, it will overflow into the communities that we are a part of.

As a mother, I desire for my children to know that they are valuable. I want them to love how God has created them, as well as appreciating the differences between themselves. Helping them appreciate one another and celebrate who they are helps them value the differences they have with others. There are practical ways to help them value other people, such as giving them opportunities to give to others, serve others, and celebrate others without receiving anything in return. These are basic components of the culture in our home, ones that my husband and I are intentional to demonstrate to them. Therefore, it is natural for our kids to see value in everyone, even someone as small as an unborn baby in the womb.

My experience is that children should not be sheltered from the truth of abortion. God can and will use our children to humble us and bring truth to the forefront when our hearts grow dull. I have seen children lead the way, exhorting adults in the community on the topic of abortion. A child's way of thinking is typically so pure and innocent that the same truths that are difficult for adults to swallow are obvious to a child. When we share (with wisdom) with children what abortion is, there is absolutely no middle ground to them. The truth of abortion so contradicts their reality of God, love, and family, that they cannot fathom why our society allows it.

All our churches and communities are comprised of amazing families who have a heart to serve, live, build godly marriages, and raise godly children. Investing in these families is an extremely wise way to spend our time and resources. In the midst of that investment, we will likely discover that some families and marriages are struggling. Despite the façade on the outside, there are likely a number of hurting and broken families in our communities. There may be newlyweds trying to find their way, and there are empty nesters struggling to find purpose in life again. Like each of us, these people need investment, encouragement, accountability, and unconditional love. We create a culture of life when we live in light and love and invest in each other. We don't have to be perfect in order to help another person in need, but we need to strive for spiritually healthy marriages and families. Then we can truly have the power and authority to bring change to our communities. Having healthy people and healthy families leads to a healthy community.

Abortion only comes to seem necessary when there's been a breakdown somewhere in the family. This breakdown, especially in the church, usually takes place in secret. It is hidden in shame, church activities, and busyness. During my work as a crisis pregnancy counselor, I witnessed this family breakdown become the life event that snowballed into a young girl seeking an abortion. In many of these cases, a healthy dating relationship has not been modeled to her. Therefore, she doesn't have healthy boundaries in relationships with men. Divorce, fatherlessness, and parents tirelessly striving for the American dream all have the power to steer a young person into the destructive direction of abortion.

The way we live and the topic of our conversations will instruct the next generation positively or negatively. What we do, the next generation will learn. An investment in families and marriages means that we begin to teach honorable parenting and to value godly marriages. This doesn't require perfection, simply striving for godliness and holiness. It requires a vulnerability to allow others to see us fail as well as succeed. Our young people need to see their father honoring and nurturing their mother. They need to feel love and acceptance in the home as well as through spiritual mothers and fathers in the church.

We must also remember that before abortion ever comes into the picture, a sexually intimate relationship or act has to have occurred. I know this is obvious, but I mention it because it seems we so often forget this. The issue begins with unhealthy relationships, and sexual behavior within those relationships. My point is that abortion is not our first problem. Do we know where our young people are? Do we know the relationships they are in? Are we supporting their wrong decisions by simply putting them on birth control? We cannot have discussions about abortion without teaching and modeling healthy relationships, including healthy sexual relationships.

Yes, we have to talk about sex in the church. Our society has no compunction against presenting sex to our young people. Sex is everywhere: the internet, movies, television shows, and social media. Our culture is obsessed with sex and presents it as thrilling and adventurous. In the church at large, we have either remained silent or communicated that sex is bad, dirty, and sinful outside of marriage. Even in the context of marriage, I am afraid we have painted the incorrect picture. We so often do not experience or communicate the sacred and passionate pursuit that a sexual relationship between a married man and woman is meant to be. Instead, our representation of it is too often boring. Which representation do you think two sixteen-year-olds are going to go for? They want adventure, so they throw out the Bible's perspective all together, or they never had the Bible's perspective to begin with. Sex *was created* to be thrilling and adventurous for married heterosexual couples; God never meant for it to be boring. He gave it to us to bring pleasure, greater intimacy, physical oneness, and of course babies. This truth is amazing, worth protecting, and worth communicating to the next generation.

Investing in marriages and families in real and authentic ways not only creates healthy sexual relationships, but also healthier people. After falling in love with Jesus and learning His Word, marriage and family investments should be at the forefront of everything we do. How can we possibly impact the culture around us without healthy relationships in our own culture? Whether it is mentorships that happen organically within our communities, or providing marriage counseling or conferences, providing a way for couples and families to find fulfillment is a crucial first step to breathing life into our community.

DISCIPLESHIP

God never intended for any of us to have to figure out life on our own. He created us to need—and to have—relationships. He desires for us to learn from one another, pour into each other, and go farther together than we could alone. One generation learning from the former is the essence of godly discipleship. Good discipleship connections and communities create godly people, godly relationships, and godly churches. When I talk about discipleship, I mean true "get up in your grill," pray it through, sacrificial relationships. Godly discipleship requires people or families giving of themselves and living life together. And we are all called to be disciples of Jesus.

Jesus is our model for our relationships with others, and He has called us to go and "make disciples of all nations" (Matthew 28:19). This is our great commission. We are meant to live life in a community with discipleship relationships. We can see this throughout the

Scriptures: Jesus and His disciples, Paul and Timothy, and Paul and all the churches he started. The community of the first church in Acts was full of sharing life and discipleship relationships.

We are all meant to learn from each other and impart to each other. It can certainly be difficult to live like this and it takes intentionality, yet it is incredibly rewarding. I am so thankful to have had this kind of godly discipleship modeled for me through the campus ministry I was a part of. I was not only in a discipleship relationship myself, but I was also equipped to offer discipleship to younger women. I met weekly for over seven years with women a little older than me who poured into me, as well as young women I poured into through prayer, Bible study, and accountability. Discipleship was an integral part of our culture. It was a natural overflow of our love for one another. It was also a requirement in order to be in any form of leadership. A value for healthy marriage, family, and intimacy with God was modeled to me and others. When you meet with that kind of consistency and with God at the center of the relationship, both people are transformed from the inside out. The principles I learned through those relationships have impacted my entire life and every other relationship I have had since then. Those discipleship relationships changed the way I view and do church, family, and marriage.

What does discipleship look like in your own life and your community of believers? What works for your community may be very different than the discipleship model I experienced. In fact, I have been involved in several other ministries, and none of them have modeled discipleship in exactly the same way. It looks different as our communities take different shapes, have different capacities, different age ranges, jobs, families, etc. When we create opportunities for discipleship in a way that fits our body of believers, we will learn each other's struggles and weaknesses as well as our strengths and gifts. When we create a culture of discipleship, we create a culture of honor. When we truly honor one another, we naturally create a culture where another's mistakes are answered with grace.

HONOR

Honoring someone is showing genuine respect for them and valuing them for who they are and who God has made them to be. I find it easy to love and honor some people in my life more than others. It's easy for me to love and honor my husband because he is amazing and because he shows the same honor to me. Other people in my life are more difficult to honor. These are the relationships that shed light onto my heart and that refine my soul. In Romans 12:9–11, Paul exhorts us to "let love be without hypocrisy. Abhor what is evil; cling to what is good. Be devoted to one another in brotherly love; give preference to one another in honor; not lagging behind in diligence, fervent in spirit, serving the Lord." This is the honor we are called to extend to others. Honor is showing respect and servanthood to those around us: no matter their age, race, socioeconomic status, sexual orientation, or their appearance or life circumstances.

A community that honors one another honors the three-year-old little boy who disrupts the service, just as much as it honors the deacon in the front of the room leading the congregation in worship. A community that honors each other honors the single mom who comes to church with her three kids, struggling to make it at all, unable to serve as much as the "perfect" married couple that serves in the church in every capacity. Do we honor our children regardless of how they act or the choices they make? Do we honor our pastors when they make decisions that we don't agree with or don't understand? Do we honor our spouse when we are among friends? These are important questions to ask when we are trying to create a culture of life in our communities.

How can we create a culture of life among ourselves when in our hearts, minds, words, and actions we are not truly honoring others? When a woman who finds herself pregnant outside of marriage lives in a community of honor and respect, she doesn't have to worry about receiving practical support and love. When a couple who want to become foster parents live in a community of honor, they don't have to worry about how their church community will respond to them bringing into the church children who might behave inappropriately.

We must bring the Kingdom of Heaven into our communities. Where the Kingdom is, the Kingdom's values will be lived out among the people. Danny Silk explains honor well in his book, *Culture of Honor: Sustaining a Supernatural Environment.* "The principle of honor states that accurately acknowledging who people are will position us to give them what they deserve and to receive the gift of who they are in our lives. Honor creates life-giving and life-promoting relationships."[22] Honor empowers people and invites the resurrection life of God to flow into them and from them. Despite this supernatural truth, treating someone honorably is not always easy when they are different from us or are hard to love. As Silk also says, "Honor is one of the most vital core values for creating a safe place where people can be free. . . . Without a core value of honor, we find that our discomfort around those who choose to live in ways that we would

22   Danny Silk, *Culture of Honor* (Shippensburg, PA: Destiny Image, 2009), 27.

not leads us to shut down their freedom."[23] If we expect to truly impact the individuals and families in our communities with truth and life, then we have to expect that God is going to bring people to us who don't look like we do or live as we do. This can be uncomfortable. If we let our own fear rule those relationships, we will never be able to sustain the revival God longs to bring. If we allow honor to be the foundation of those relationships, God is free to move. This is the way we create a culture of life in our communities, and it starts from the top down.

SHEPHERDS & LEADERS

My husband and I have been given the responsibility to love, teach, and lead our children. We want to honor them as well as lead them into the principles of God's kingdom. We want them to have the freedom to succeed as well as fail, knowing that we are one hundred percent for them. We also want to impart wisdom to them in practical areas of life, including the harder topics of discussion that will ultimately arise as our relationships with them mature. We recognize that we have a choice. We can either teach and model godliness to them, or they will learn the way of the world from someone else. Our kids are growing up in a culture where truth has been muddied. It is my husband's and my responsibility to teach truth to them. We cannot afford for them to be rocked and swayed by the world while never hearing truth from us.

I see our position on abortion in the church the same way. If, as shepherds and leaders, we are not talking about abortion to our congregations, to our youth groups, or to our Bible study members,

---

23   Danny Silk, *Keep Your Love On* (Shippensburg, PA: Destiny Image, 2009), 160.

who will? If we don't, someone else will, and the opinions that will come from Hollywood, books, friends, friends' parents, teachers, and politicians will often be quite different from the truth we know to be true. Our children will learn from someone, and that is exactly what has happened already in many cases. The church has not been the parent teaching the child about the important issues of life. We have kept silent and so have allowed the world to mold the opinions of the next generation. The next thing we know, one-fourth of the women in our nation are having abortions.

We desperately need leaders and shepherds who teach truth and who are not afraid to create conversations about the hard issues. We all have to take responsibility for the actions of "the church" because we *are* the Church. The Church is not a building with fancy carpet and pews. The Church is me and you. Creating a culture of life within it begins at the top with intentional leaders taking responsibility for the actions of the church, and speaking wisdom and discernment into the places where we have been deceived.

Creating a culture of life is about loving each other and the people whom God brings to us. We must believe and live out the truth that we are no better than the next person, no matter their mistakes or life situation. This is what it means to be pro-life. When followers of Jesus become who we say we are and who we are called to be, we will set the standard for the world around us. When we reflect Christ, the world will be attracted to us. Women who are struggling within our walls as well as outside our walls will have a safe place to come home to. I pray that all of our communities will become abortion-free communities as we disciple, honor, and shepherd well the lives God has entrusted to us.

Chapter Four

GAINING HEAVEN'S PERSPECTIVE

My concern is not whether God is on our side;
my greatest concern is to be on God's side,
for God is always right.

—Abraham Lincoln

BRINGING HEAVEN TO EARTH IS one of the primary roles of the Church. We have the honor of being the hands and feet of Jesus and presenting Him to those around us. But we can do this well only when we understand His perspective, when our hearts beat with His. He looks for friends who are willing to listen diligently to Him and then to act according to His will. Discovering Heaven's perspective on abortion has led me to share my story, to walk into the ministry opportunities I have been given, and to write this book. When we gain the heart of the Lord, we are always compelled by love to pray and act. When we get a taste of His emotions, they become impossible to "move on" from.

Abortion is not a cause I have merely "taken up." Being pro-life is not a social justice movement that I have joined, nor am I calling anyone else to jump on the bandwagon. Creating a culture of life and love for God's creations is a way of life. I have often spoken with pastors and ministry leaders who are overwhelmed by the truth of abortion and who are trying to determine the next step for those they lead. Leaders do not want to simply add another program for their community to join. I appreciate that, so my answer to this perplexity is simple. When we simply present the truth about abortion and the truth about God, followers of Jesus will instinctively begin to pray and to be compelled by love. We must simply be willing to begin the conversation, no matter the consequences, and to care about the things God cares about. What He leads us to do next will be a natural outflow of those first steps. When we meditate on His words and ask Him what He wants us to do, He is faithful to tell us.

> The issue of abortion is so near to God's heart that I firmly believe that He is calling *many* believers to act practically . . .

The issue of abortion is so near to God's heart that I firmly believe that He is calling *many* believers to act practically, to get on their knees in prayer, to lead ministries, to take in children through adoption and foster care, and also to love the women and men harmed by abortion. The question is, are we hearing Him? And when we hear Him, do we act? Do we step into the water ready to swim the long distance race? When we are compelled by His love, we find ourselves beckoned and engulfed by something. We cannot escape it, and we instinctively move forward before our feet make the decision to move. This is the nature of the love of God. His love for all creation is the topic of conversation in Heaven. He is happy to let us in on that conversation, when and if we are willing to join.

God—who is outside of time, before all things, and after all things—saw fit to create Man in His image and His likeness. This world was created in His pleasure and for the purpose of relationship with man (Genesis 1:26), and He chose you and me to be on the earth in this sweet and yet urgent time. His story of redemption is still unfolding, and I believe we are at a climax. It is the most adventurous, passionate, and meaningful ride we will ever jump on. Regardless of what unfolds in the earth around us today, tomorrow, or in the next twenty years, the most eternal and valuable way that we can spend our life is right up next to God: learning His nature, His ways, and His desires.

There are often difficult situations surrounding any abortion decision, but it is extremely important that we have the wisdom of God, not the wisdom of man, to bring into those situations. I watch the demeanor of a young girl change as the "pregnant" line shows up on a pregnancy test. I can see the fear and almost taste the shame many of them take on, yet every time, I have to believe God for His divine intervention. I expect God's divine intervention because of His great love for two individuals, the mother and her baby. It was and still is my job to help her see and experience the truth: not by preaching to her, but by living out the ways of the Kingdom toward her. It can be difficult to walk out what we know to be true, but standing on a strong foundation of truth keeps us focused on truth in complex and potentially devastating life situations.

In Heaven's eyes, choosing life or death for another human being is not up for debate. It is not a political issue. It is a God issue. It is a creation issue, no matter how small or hidden His creation is. We need His eyes to see past the circumstances and begin to see this issue from Heaven's perspective. When we see people as God's created ones, it brings His value for their life to the forefront as the top priority, worth protecting beyond what we can see, feel, taste, and sense. I want to be those outside eyes that I needed someone to be for me when I was a scared, pregnant teenager. We have to remind women who they are, who they were created to be, and who they are loved by. When they can believe the truth that they are loved, it will change their life. Isolation will lose the battle to belonging. Fear will be defeated by faith. Devastation will be replaced with hope. These truths win the battle for life, for both mother and baby.

Our present circumstances, whatever they are, are temporary, but learning the depth of who we are and our purpose in life is eternal. As hard as it can be to understand in the moment, choosing an abortion is only a temporary "fix" to a grander and more complex story. Suggesting an abortion to a woman is a cop-out. It is easy for us. We can walk away when it is over. This is what Planned Parenthood does on a daily basis. Then they leave the woman in pain, with her real problems unchanged and her real needs unmet. It takes a hero to suggest that a woman become a parent, and then to provide her assistance, holding her hand on the road to adoption, or being willing to open our home to her and her child.

GOD'S CREATIVITY

A mother's womb is one of the most fascinating places in the universe, in my humble opinion. I'm a childbirth educator, so perhaps I am a little biased, but the more I discover and learn about this hidden place, the more I fall in love with God as our Creator. I imagine God getting out His paintbrush and preparing His hands to mold His next handiwork, His heart beating with expectation. It is simply astounding what takes place in a short nine-month period beginning from the moment of conception and throughout the first trimester.

This sweet time, as God is laying the foundation of the child's life and first revealing to a mother the gift within her, is when the majority of abortions take place in our nation. According to the Guttmacher Institute, one-third of all abortions occur within the first 6 weeks of gestation, and 89% of all abortions performed occur within the first 12 weeks of gestation.[24] Although abortion providers often use this statistic to proclaim their morality, this time is also when miracles are taking place. During the first 12 weeks, the baby's unique DNA has already been laid: the blueprint that will dictate the "beat of their drum" throughout the rest of their life. The baby's heart begins to beat, brain waves can be recorded, and clear facial features can be seen, such as ears, eyes, nose, and even eyebrows. These are just a few of the amazing developments taking place within the first trimester of pregnancy. God's creative ways are truly extraordinary, and I am extremely thankful that science continues to reveal more and more of His great architecture. When we look inside the womb of a woman who is 12-weeks pregnant, it is impossible to deny that life exists within it. Therefore, is morality truly on our side when we choose to end a heartbeat that has beat for only a few weeks rather than seventy years? Is one person more worthy of saving than another?

---

24   "Induced Abortion in the United States" fact sheet, Guttmacher Institute, May 2016, www.guttmacher.org/fact-sheet/induced-abortion-united-states#4/.

It is a wondrous thing that God, in His infinite wisdom, has chosen to trust and bless us weak, broken, and unfaithful humans with the privilege of carrying His greatest gift to the earth: another human. Many times as I carried my second child I was overwhelmed by the trust God put in me: to manage the immense task of carrying a young person in my body. Soon I would hold her, protect her, care for her, and disciple her. My husband and I both felt the weight of that reality. Sometimes we were very excited about that responsibility, and other times we were completely terrified and felt dangerously inadequate. This was another life, and we were responsible for stewarding it.

As my husband and I fill more seats in our minivan, I keep coming back to this truth. *God* created *my children*: as crazy and precious as they are—He created them. He knows them backwards and forwards. He knows the number of their days on the earth. He knows if and who they will marry, and the children they will have. In those moments when I feel lost and ill-equipped to shepherd them, I can rest in the knowledge that He is not: He has given them gifts to express His heart to the world and He will prosper them. My job as a parent is simply to call their gifts forth and provide a little guidance along the way.

The Scriptures make crystal clear, in numerous places, how much value God places on the unborn child. He not only places us in our mother's womb, but He meticulously forms and molds us. Even though children in the womb might be hidden from our eyes, they are not hidden from His. In Psalm 139 King David rejoices, "My frame was not hidden from You, When I was made in secret, and skillfully wrought in the depths of the earth; Your eyes have seen my unformed substance; And in Your book were all written the days that were ordained for me, when as yet there was not one of them." God's eyes were on us even when we were still unformed. So when we stop the heartbeat of an unborn child, we are ending one of God's dreams.

Choosing to live out God's love for all His created ones has the power to revolutionize the way that we live. God has called each one of us (even from the womb, David says) to live out a divine destiny. We read of multiple accounts in Scripture where He invites parents to join in the protection and nurturing of this purpose. For example, God set apart Samson (Judges 13:5), Samuel (1 Samuel 1:11), and John the Baptist (Luke 1:15) as unique individuals who were to be consecrated as Nazarites. God revealed the names and destiny of John the Baptist and Jesus to their parents before they were in their mothers' wombs. God even filled John the Baptist with His Holy Spirit while in the womb of his mother, Elizabeth (Luke 1:41). As an unborn baby, John leapt in the presence of his long-awaited Savior. God also reminded Jeremiah of his commission from the womb (Jeremiah 1:5), and revealed to Rebekah the destiny of her sons, Jacob and Esau.

Yet even Jesus' arrival on the Earth did not come in the midst of perfect circumstances. Mary and Joseph were not yet married. Mary was young, likely only a teenager, and the only place for Jesus to be born was a dirty trough among animals. His birth was glorious because of who He was, but the circumstances were not in the least glorious; in fact, overall they were awful. So why do we insist that all the circumstances have to be perfect now before we will welcome a baby into the world? This is the same demonic deception that led to the founding of Planned Parenthood. Instead of turning a blind eye to this fact, as followers of Jesus we are called to stand up and say 'No!' as an innocent child's execution date is put on the calendar of the local abortion clinic. Yet tragically, even among Christian women, a mother's womb is one of the most dangerous places to live today. The death rate in the womb is horrifying.

And think of all that we are losing! I often wonder about characteristics of God that we have yet to discover because He longed to reveal them through a younger brother or sister who did not survive the womb. I think about Earth's discoveries and gems that have yet to be uncovered because God had a perfect and great plan to reveal those things through someone who was aborted. What is still to come? Our political speeches may continue to end with "God Bless America," but we are refusing to accept the untold blessings that God wants to give us through the wombs of American women.

MERCY TRIUMPHS

Because of God's love, we have been given the free will to make choices. God does not force us to walk in righteousness, nor does He force us to walk in love with Him. And in many ways we have all, like wayward children, chosen unwisely and have walked apart from Him. Children also make messes, and we adults have made quite a mess of our world. Yet sometimes the mess must lead to real consequences. My young children are professional mistake-makers, and sometimes I have to let them suffer the consequences of their choices. It hurts me as their parent to watch them learn painfully, but I know that this is sometimes required in order for them to learn wisdom and to sharpen their character.

As our good and wise Father, God also sometimes allows us to make our mistakes and learn from them. Many of these mistakes break His heart and have real and devastating consequences. After my abortion, God allowed me to feel deep pain and sorrow because I had ignored His kind convictions and divine stop signs on the path to my horrible decision. (He even tried to stop me as I was in the clinic preparing for the abortion.)

There was absolutely no part of God's heart that condoned my decision to take the life of my child, yet He still loves me and has never forsaken me. He gave me free will and the choice to love and follow Him; therefore, He allowed me to walk down a road that not only broke His heart, but would soon also break my own heart. He allowed me to reach the end of myself so that I could find Him. I am thankful for His unfailing mercy in the many rock-bottom moments of my life that followed my abortion. His mercy brought forth righteousness and wisdom in my life; like Job, without His divine intervention I would surely have perished.

Whether the choices are made by an individual, a community, or an entire nation, God will allow the consequences and judgment to come that will bring the most people to salvation and bring the glory that is due Him. The prophet Isaiah reminds us that "when the earth experiences Your judgments, the inhabitants of the world learn righteousness" (Isaiah 26:9). God's discipline and correction is intended to help us choose righteousness. God's discipline is always for our good. His discipline reminds us that we are His sons and daughters (Hebrews 12:8). Paul reminds us that, in the moment, no discipline seems joyful, but sorrowful; yet to those who have been trained by it, afterwards it yields the peaceful fruit of righteousness. (Hebrews 12:11). Yet without massive repentance, I fear what the discipline of God upon America will look like for our crime of legalizing and sanctioning the murder of over fifty million babies.

The abortion industry in America is a cash-cow, and our federal tax dollars support it. Aborted babies are used in vaccines and medical research, as well as material things that we use every day—and without us even knowing it. Countless stores and organizations to which we give our money support the abortion industry. The blood of the innocents has inundated our society. We are choosing death for profit, and this is no small matter. The Scriptures say "Woe to him who builds a city with bloodshed and founds a town with violence!" (Habakkuk 2:12). And when a nation refuses to repent, the Lord says, "I will give you over to bloodshed, and bloodshed will pursue you" (Ezekiel 35:6).

I do not enjoy preaching doom and judgment, but we desperately need to feel His conviction and understand the severity of the choices we are making. We cannot continue making destructive choices without eventually suffering the consequences. The Bible clearly tells us that "the life of the flesh is in the blood" (Leviticus 17:11) and "whoever sheds man's blood, by man his blood shall be shed, for in the image of God He made man (Genesis 9:6). God does not condone abortion. He does not condone the shedding of innocent blood, no matter the circumstance. His Word is clear. There will be a day when the cover-up of innocent bloodshed in our trash cans and back rooms of abortion clinics will be revealed (Isaiah 26:11), and the blood will be on our hands.

America's situation reminds me of the story of Cain and Abel. Cain became jealous of his brother Abel, and in a fit of jealousy and rage, he killed Abel. The Lord then visited Cain to question him. "What have you done? The voice of your brother's blood is crying to Me from the ground" (Genesis 4:10). God knew what had happened (and surely Cain knew that God would know), yet when God questioned him, Cain brazenly responded, "I don't know. Am I my brother's keeper?" (Genesis

4:9). We are understandably horrified by Cain's actions and attitude, but is America—even Christian America—any better? Over a million innocent children are being aborted every year in America, mostly due to our own selfishness and our desire for a better material life. We then try to hide our sin and believe that we can simply move on.

This is exactly what I did. Even when I came face-to-face with the truth, I tried to pretend that it didn't exist. For years I mourned the trauma surrounding my abortion, but I had never realized that I was mourning the loss of my baby. I covered it up, just as Cain did, until the Lord in His kindness confronted me. When I least expected it, in the corner of a room in the Dirksen Senate Building in Washington D.C., God confronted me. I had joined about fifty other people for a time of worship and strategic prayer for America. Though the atmosphere in the room was electric, I chose a spot in the corner to meet with God. With my face on the floor (God often chooses to meet me there), I heard a whisper in my ear. I don't know if it was audible to anyone else there, but it sounded to me as if it would have been. His voice was clear, and His words wrecked me.

"Her name is Hannah," He said.

"Whose name is Hannah?" I asked.

"Your baby. I named her Hannah," He responded.

His words pierced my heart. I could barely breathe. Not only was God speaking to my heart, which was incredible, but His words brought clarity to a mystery I had been puzzled by for some time. Several years before that moment, I had begun to study the first two chapters of the book of 1 Samuel. These chapters give us a short glimpse into the life of one of the most amazing and mysterious women we meet in the Scriptures. Her name was Hannah. I felt drawn to study her life. At times during my study it felt as if God had breathed those pages into His Word just for me, and I was allured by their mystery. Suddenly, in that moment on the floor of the Dirksen Building, my pursuit made sense. God had set me up. He had wooed me, pursued me, and introduced me to this woman in the Scriptures, all to help me understand that the baby I had aborted had a name, and her name was Hannah. Her heavenly Father had named her before the beginning of time. He had molded her, and He had a purpose for her.

I had "moved on" after my abortion, but in doing so I had forgotten my daughter. I did mourn her life, but I had also pushed the thought of her far away from me, because the pain cut too deep. Now I wept, as God told me all about my little Hannah. I could see her in my mind's eye. She is beautiful, she is with Jesus, and she is full of life. And now, for the first time in my life, the thought of my daughter brought joy to my heart instead of pain. When I said her name, I smiled. In the midst of a prayer meeting to pray for our nation and the ending of abortion, I was taken hostage by my own prayers. I learned that day that prayer not only has the power to change the course of world history, but even the course of our own history.

My baby has a name, and so do the millions of other children who have been aborted. They have a name in Heaven, and their lives matter. They matter to God, and they should matter to us. They are just as deserving of life as you and I are. In our "enlightened" society this truth is not politically correct, but as followers of Jesus we must study the Word of God and become consumed with His truth. Politically correct or not, His truth is part of His plan of mercy for our nation. It is time for us to live out the perspective of Heaven.

Chapter Five

LABELS, SECRETS, AND LIES

She had not known the weight until she felt the freedom.

—Nathaniel Hawthorne, *The Scarlet Letter*

CAN A WOMAN BE FORGIVEN after having an abortion? I must have asked myself this question over a thousand times. Had I committed a sin that eliminated all opportunity to enter into God's kingdom? Had I severed my chances at favor, joy, and delight? I didn't see how I could ever find His joy again. Honestly, I'm not sure that I had ever truly felt His joy, but I longed for it. But I wondered if those days of longing for a life that brought meaning and purpose were only in vain, after what I had done. I believed that not only had God cast me to the wind, but my parents surely would as well, once they discovered the real me. As for my youth pastor and college ministry leaders, I thought it was best for them to never know. I saw no benefit in revealing anything about my present or my past that might give them a closer look at the real person hiding behind my skin.

I wore a badge of shame. I was clothed in cloaks of guilt. I felt that I had traveled too far into darkness to ever reach forgiveness. It was much easier to turn and run in the other direction. Choosing an abortion was against my nature, my ideals, and my values, yet after my crippling decision, being a woman in favor of "choice" was the only way I could find what seemed like a glimpse of freedom in my life. I was like Hester in Nathaniel Hawthorne's famous book, *The Scarlet Letter.* As Hester wore her large letter 'A' for *Adultery*, I wore an invisible letter 'A' for *Abortion*. Hawthorne writes of Hester, "The scarlet letter was her passport into regions where other women dared not tread. Shame, Despair, Solitude! These had been her teachers—stern and wild ones— and they had made her strong, but taught her much amiss."

I found freedom—or at least a semblance of it—in my 'A.' The shame of my hidden sin became my teacher. It taught me to be bold for "choice." It taught me to be angry. It taught me to give up. Wearing the label was my way of giving in to the demons of my past. They were far too strong to fight, I thought. At least that way I could stop fighting all the time: fighting for joy and hoping desperately for forgiveness. But just as for Hester, for post-abortive women (and actually for all pro-choice women) that so-called freedom is no freedom at all. My feelings made me strong, but they taught me amiss. I started living as if I had hit the mark, yet I was completely missing the bull's-eye. I had lost sight of truth.

Today there are millions of women in our society—and in our churches—who feel exactly as I felt. They are walking around with an invisible label sewn to their blouse. Many of these women have fallen prey to the label and so have lived in silence for ten, twenty, or even more years because of it. Whether it is actively projected or merely perceived, that label is present. In an effort to hide their pain, many women have taken off their fancy high-heeled shoes and replaced them with war boots. Fighting the fight for "choice"—or simply the fight to feel alive—has become their fate. Perhaps this sinful societal label is only a figment of their imagination, yet surveys reveal that many women choose abortion because of this perceived judgment from others. Whether the judgment is real or perceived doesn't really matter, though: the consequences are the same. Yet just as Jesus did with the woman caught in adultery, we Christians must follow our Lord's example and work to redeem the person and their situation. We must make the sacrificial effort to change both the judgment and the consequences.

One of the first things I learned in my post-abortion counseling and ministry training was always, no matter what anyone said to me, to keep a poker face. So I learned to listen, and I learned to respond with empathy and authentic love regardless of what anyone brought to me. Countless times while working in campus ministry, young college girls would come up to me at the altar after our Wednesday night service and tell me of the horrible situations they were in or the terrible choices they had made. Sometimes it took all my self-control not to look shocked or react to what they were saying with "preacher words." Regardless of what the person was telling me, I learned to pray and ask God for His opinion of her and her situation.

I can only imagine how difficult it might be for my husband and me to react this way with our children when they are older. Will we be able to truly listen to them, instead of reacting out of our own fear, need for control, or anger? I have friends with teenagers who have come to them with some of the most worrisome and horrible choices.

I can well believe that reacting in authentic love and calmly listening to one's teenagers, rather than preaching at them, can be extremely difficult; I hope that I can manage it.

Truly listening, not merely reacting, is hard. We are human, after all, and so we are easily caught off guard. Thankfully, God is never surprised. When someone in your church confesses that they have had an abortion, He is not shocked. Of course, their announcement will probably be shocking and possibly even devastating, but women and men who have experienced the trauma from abortion have to be able to come to their fellow believers for help. Families who have experienced abortion need a place of refuge and not a place of judgment. When I think back on my choice to have an abortion, one of the things that, tragically, made it a little easier was that I knew no one in my church would ever ask me about it, because abortion was never mentioned in my church. I knew that it would be easy to hide. I thought this was a good thing.

On the other hand, I sometimes wonder if my choice would have been different, or even harder, if I had been part of a church that not only talked about abortion but also openly spoke against it, and even fought for the ending of it. What if I had been a member of a church that was actively pro-life, and I fell in the middle of the battle? What if I heard my pastor preach against abortion, encourage us to give and donate our time to pro-life efforts, and even pray openly for the ending of abortion? To be honest, I think it would have been even harder to come forward about my unplanned pregnancy in that church than it was for me in the church that never took a stance. The power of shame could have been that much stronger—unless the church also put their feet and prayers into action. It is always hard to confess sin, but if my church had had a history of helping pregnant women and babies, then at least I would have grown up seeing them loving and forgiving and being merciful to their fellow sinners, and I might have felt a bit more comfortable confessing my own sin.

My hope is that we all discover how we can truly help women who are considering an abortion, as well as women in our midst who have already had abortions. Thankfully, the number of abortions in America are slowly decreasing and many abortion clinics are closing. That is exciting, but we have to look backward as well as forward. We so often charge ahead with spears held high, hoping to save hundreds of babies, mothers, and fathers from the pain of abortion. Unfortunately we also often assume that the people needing rescuing are somewhere "out there." We must stop for a moment and look behind us, in front, and on every side. Then we can see the hundreds who have already fallen in the midst of the battle, or who are bruised and at risk of falling. If we don't do this, our army will dwindle and weaken, and we will ultimately lose the battle altogether. I challenge you (as well as myself), as we pray and seek God on how to create a culture of life, not to forget those who are hurting now and need help now in our midst.

When someone we love falls, it can be extremely difficult to not view them differently, especially if we ourselves are hurt by their decision. Sometimes it may feel impossible to forgive them and get over, or overlook, their issue. But as followers of Jesus, we are called to be a place of refuge

> As followers of Jesus, our demonstrations of compassion and mercy are supposed to match His.

for the people in our communities who are broken and hurting, not a place of condemnation and labeling.

Because of the shame surrounding abortion, even if we aren't intending to judge or condemn the person, much of the time they will assume that we are. Therefore our demonstrations of compassion and mercy must go above and beyond the norm; in fact, they are supposed to match His. We cannot allow ourselves to be so naive as to believe that simply talking about abortion one day per year, and saying that we are available if someone needs help, is enough. If we truly want to become a place of refuge for the hurting people around us, then we must be willing to expend the effort necessary to create a culture of life and love. Building a reputation that people can trust requires extending our hands to them over a period of time.

I encourage you to stop and consider for a moment what you would think if someone you are close to, perhaps someone in your family or church, confessed an abortion to you. Would you be shocked? Would you be hurt? How would you move forward? How would it feel to learn that it took place twenty years ago and you are the first to know about it? As sad as it is to contemplate, according to abortion statistics it is likely that any of us could find ourselves in this scenario—if we are known as a safe person to confide in. It is vital, therefore, that we consider how we would respond to such an admission of guilt. It is all too easy for us to say that we would love unconditionally and support one of those "other people." The reality is that many of "those other" women are our mothers, our sisters, our friends, and even our ministry leaders.

Of course we must acknowledge the full reality of what abortion is. We must never condone abortion, yet at the same time we must find a way not to create a secret box of shame for those who have had abortions or those who find themselves in an unexpected pregnancy outside of marriage. I think the answer to this dilemma is an individual answer. We must search our own hearts, put ourselves in the other person's shoes, and not give in to the fear or shock or anger that can easily surface when someone we know, someone in our cozy little circle, turns out to be one of "them." Especially when what they desperately need is our help and our love.

I sometimes wonder what we are so afraid of? Why do we condemn and put labels on people, including women and men involved in abortion decisions? Of course, it is often easier to push away someone else's pain, or even (in an effort at self-preservation) the pain we ourselves might feel because of another's choice. It can be easier to simply carry on with life and ignore the hard realities in the lives of those around us. Those realities might beckon us to journey down a path we don't feel comfortable walking. Those hard realities might cause us to give of ourselves more than we are eager to give, or to take a stance that could damage our reputation. We all encounter these temptations every day. I encounter them in the grocery store when I know that someone could use a kind word or a helping hand. I see the need, but I'm in a rush to get in and out with my three crazy kids before they knock down a tower of cans. If I stop and help that stranger, my kids will surely become human bulldozers, so I decide that it's not worth the hassle. We can all be tempted at times to wander into the warm pool of self-preservation, but we must say 'No!' to our comfort when it would lead to another person drowning.

I've encountered this temptation many times in ministry settings, when I've been (usually politely) asked not to mention abortion.

I've been questioned about my motive if I say that I am planning to mention it. At first it was hard for me not to be offended by this scrutiny, but I've come to realize that the fear of saying the word "ABORTION" is in many of us. It's a scary word. It has become a political word. I can't say that I blame a pastor or a friend for not wanting a conversation to go down that road, because to be honest, when someone would learn that I was writing a book, sometimes I was tempted to keep the topic a secret. Sometimes it's simply hard to have those conversations. I understand. Yet, I still wonder, why *has* abortion become such a bad word in *church*, of all places? Are we trying to protect people from a sudden avalanche of shame that will fall from Heaven the moment the word is spoken, or do we just not want people in the pews to squirm in embarrassment? It might be a little of both.

Yes, there is wisdom and appropriate timing for everything, but that's not what I'm referring to. I'm talking about the times we deliberately silence the truth even though we know it could set someone free or prevent them from experiencing pain. We silence the truth because we don't want to deal with the mess it could create. In situations that we personally find difficult or painful, we too often allow the battle to become against the person in pain rather than against the enemy causing the pain. We restrict the Holy Spirit from speaking truth and ministering to the deep places of people's souls because we want control of the room, the retreat, the small group, or the conference. But this is nothing less than self-preservation. Many of our attempts to be politically correct and relevant are actually selfishness—and disobedience to the Lord. Are we trying to be best friends with seekers or best friends with God? We cannot always be both.

There are women and men sitting in our church pews who have hidden an abortion decision for ten, twenty, or thirty years because they are terrified to confess that unforgivable "bad word." They have been silenced. We have to be willing to initiate and sustain a conversation with them, come what may. The consequences if we don't "speak and let speak" are far too great. We cannot afford those consequences. The more that we silence the truth and shrink back in fear, the more we will unintentionally project harmful labels on these people. Abortion will continue to be the elephant in the room that we ignore. The more we try to "protect" our people from the pain of talking about abortion, the longer we condemn some of them to remain in perhaps the deepest pain they have ever experienced.

SECRETS

Probably all of us have struggled with secret sin at some point in our life, whether large or small. Confession and transparency can be difficult even when we have a safe community to unveil ourselves to. We all have a desire to be fully known, yet how many of us allow ourselves to experience the pleasure in it? Not all secrets are bad or even need to be revealed to everyone, but there are many times when we make bad choices, think thoughts, and even live disguised lives deliberately among those we love. A long-kept secret has the power to take over and create an identity or a label. When we decide to keep a sinful act in hiding, immediately the door to the enemy opens. His lies rush in like a flood and he begins to chip away at our relationships.

This is exactly what is taking place with many post-abortive women, especially in the Church. The choice has been made. The act has been carried out, and immediately we hear and choose to listen to the voice of the enemy that tells us, "don't tell anyone." We buy into the lies, and they eat away at every part of our being. The lies spread like a cancer throughout us and find a home. Abortion, adultery, divorce, abuse, and self-destructive behavior all can have this effect when kept in the dark. Mold and mildew grow in the dark places. Life withers without sunlight and the food of truth.

In my experience, women and men after abortions who intend on keeping it a secret also slowly erect a mental and emotional vault, or lockbox, to hide it in. That secret is kept in the deepest and darkest place of who they are. Unfortunately, much of the time, their heart also gets thrown into the vault along with the secret. I successfully boarded up my heart with as much wood and nails as I could find after my abortion. I dug a deep ditch for that secret and hid it away quite skillfully and purposely. I assured myself that there was absolutely no way that anyone could ever discover it, no matter how hard they searched. I vowed it would never see the daylight in any relationship I ever entered. And so my heart was boarded up as well. It had to be. I knew that if I allowed someone to touch my heart tenderly with unconditional love, they might get close enough to actually see the lockbox within me and wonder what might be inside. I questioned my ability to keep it hidden if anyone ever purposely searched for it. My secret hurt so bad, that I thought I might accidentally let it out in my desperation to be loved and accepted. But I was desperate to not let that happen. I was so fearful of my reputation being destroyed and being labeled and condemned, I decided that I had to keep my shameful secret hidden at all costs.

Secrets can have that kind of power. We give them power to run our lives and twist our sentences. Our secrets also project an illusion to us. We convince ourselves that our secret is locked away forever and no one will ever suspect. We believe that we can go on with our lives as normal, yet that is never possible. Those we love may not know what the secret is, yet they will know that something is different about us. Our demeanor changes. I think about the not-so-innocent faces I see on my own children after they have committed an act of guilty pleasure. Thankfully, they are still young, so most of their sinful actions are nothing worse than stealing another cookie out of the kitchen or ripping up their sibling's favorite book after an argument. They go in secret, commit their act, and come out with the cutest little guilty faces. I may not know what they've done, but I immediately know they've done something worth an investigation!

Some of us are better at hiding secrets than others. We may have even mastered the art, but the sealed vault is still only an illusion. The cancer will spread. It might not be obvious to others at first, but eventually the devastation on the inside will make its way to the surface. Our secrets can manifest as anger, shame, guilt, or even physical illness. Our relationships will change, or remain only surface-level. The heart connections we had with our children will be broken. Our marriages might self-destruct. Those around us might not know precisely what is wrong or different, but it will be obvious that something is.

We must recognize the severity of a secret like a hidden abortion and how incredibly difficult it can be for someone to confess it. It is unlike a simple poor choice we might be accustomed to confessing to loved ones throughout the day. When we have an altar call, for example, for women and men involved in abortion, we must recognize that when someone is brave enough to come forward and confess, they are handing you the key to a private lockbox. The lockbox might have been sitting in the dark place of their heart for years. You might be the only one who has been given the key. It requires careful handling, sincerity, and willingness to help such a person. We cannot have someone reveal a secret of that magnitude to us—and then just leave them there in their mess. Removing harmful labels and damaging secrets requires shining light and truth on them. Secrets are extremely powerful, and bringing light into them can be a delicate and also an extremely freeing experience that transcends every part of someone's life.

When we reveal a heavy secret or ask someone to come forward to confess one, our request has to be married to wisdom. If you are carrying a secret, it is important to remember that not everyone needs to know your secret. If you are ministering to someone who wants to share a secret with you, especially one such as abortion or sexual sin, you need to know if you are truly the proper person to handle their confession. I love what Beth Moore says in her study, *Sacred Secrets*: We should have "authenticity with all, transparency with most, and intimacy with some."[25] Not everyone needs to know everything about us, especially intimate knowledge of us. It can be tempting, especially in times when we experience God's freedom, to announce our greatest sins from the rooftops for all to know. This is unwise, though, especially when our confessor may themself not be fully healed. We must be sensitive to the Lord's leading as to the appropriate time and person for sharing our secret.

God does want to bring His light into the secret places of our hearts. He wants to speak truth and heal us of the emotional cancer

25   Beth Moore, *Sacred Secrets: A Living Proof Live Experience* (Nashville, TN: Lifeway, 2013), 46.

they have caused. This can take time, but as we trust Him, keep ourselves humble before Him, and link arms with other trusted believers, our self-erected prison vault can be transformed into a beautiful secret place of intimacy. It is like coming home. Our frame was not hidden from Him when we were made in the secret place (Psalm 139:15). He already knows us. He already knew the secret was there and He desires for us to feel the warmth of dwelling in the secret place of His tent (Psalm 27:5) and the shelter of His shadow (Psalm 91:1).

As the body of Christ, we can lead those who entrust us with the knowledge of their past mistakes to the Lord and His shelter. After someone has been hiding in secret shame for years, there is nothing more liberating and healing than to discover God's amazing acceptance and forgiveness! The enemy tries to convince all of us that we are not worthy of this forgiveness, while God has His arms opened wide, just waiting for us. It is an amazing honor when we are given the opportunity to wrap our arms around someone to bring forth that comfort to an open wound ready to receive ointment.

LIES

When someone's life has been founded upon labels and secrets, lies about their identity can then grow like weeds and take over. We can begin to believe that we are someone different than the person we truly are. We might believe lies from the enemy about another person that causes us to see them differently than God sees them. The devil is a liar. He is the Father of lies (John 8:44). He knows that if he can get us to believe lies about ourselves or others, he can chip away at our identity and our God-ordained destiny. On the other hand, it is impossible for God to lie (Hebrews 6:18). When we allow the light of truth to penetrate our soul, this opens us up to hear and believe the truth about who we really are.

It is common for women and men who have had an abortion or been involved in one to believe that they have committed the unforgiveable sin. Then it becomes easier for them to take on an identity saturated in lies. They may believe they are murderers who do not deserve a future. They may believe they are liars who do not deserve to be trusted. The enemy's lies cause women to believe they can choose the destiny of their child. They believe that choosing their child's death will lead to a full, happy, and normal life for themselves. Later, after their abortion, many women immediately realize the lie they believed, yet more lies come flooding in, kicking them when they are already down.

The abortion industry was soaked in lies from its beginning. The abortion decision begins with the lie that a baby is not a person, but is instead merely a "personal choice." Those lies have been compounded and have deceived millions of people. Due to the power of entrenched demonic deception over this issue, defeating the enemy's lies is one of the toughest battles women and men face after going through an abortion.

But together, and with Heaven's help, we can overcome the lies that women and men have come to believe about themselves. We can overcome the lies that we have believed about them, and we can overcome the lies flowing through our church doors from the abortion industry. Many of us have been deceived. But Christians have access to the truth, and the truth sets people free!

Chapter Six

SEVENTY TIMES SEVEN

The woman left her water pot and went into the city and said to the men:
"Come, see a man who told me all the things that I have done."

John 4:27–29

EMBRACING LIES, SECRETS, AND LABELS was easier for me than receiving God's free healing ointment of forgiveness, because I expected rejection and disapproval from others. But my life of deception became like a house containing nothing but bare, blank walls. Pictures of beautiful memories and dreams slowly came down, until one day an unexpected moment from Heaven slipped into my life. Suddenly, without my consent, my secret exploded out of my mouth as a close friend was praying for me. Love from the others around me slowly extinguished the lie that I would be rejected if I were fully known, so I took a chance. One by one, I relinquished control over each nail that held together my prison, and the walls of my heart were once again adorned with vibrant colors. Forgiveness flowed freely into its open and empty spaces.

Forgiveness requires truth. The lies must be torn down so that truth can reflect back to us in every mirror around us. Forgiveness begins with believing God's thoughts about us. What He says about us is not changed by what we have done or not done: the good, the bad, and the ugly. There is nothing that we can do to make Him love us any less or any more. When we focus on the Cross, everything else becomes secondary. Jesus is glorified and suddenly our sin, even our worst sin, is diminished in comparison with His sacrifice.

> Forgiveness begins with believing God's thoughts about us. There is nothing that we can do to make Him love us any less or any more.

Nevertheless, receiving forgiveness can be a difficult journey. The lies hold on to us tightly . . . or perhaps we hold onto them? There were many things about forgiveness that confused me and caused me to shy away from it. First of all, I thought that perhaps I had a wrong idea of what forgiveness really was. And God's forgiveness seemed too good to be true. Could His love really cover a multitude of sins? Surely there was something I had to do to earn it. Surely there were still records of wrongs recorded in His book? Maybe He could forgive others, but the stain of *my* sin seemed impenetrable. I would have to take a chance to find out . . . but was the chance worth the risk? Could I stand the pain if I was wrong?

I also wondered if forgiveness meant that I had to forget the wrongs that had been done to me. I knew enough to know that if God were willing to forgive me, I was also called to forgive my wrongdoers. Forgiving them seemed to be a sign of weakness, though, and I wasn't ready to issue a pardon to someone who had hurt me so terribly. Holding onto anger and bitterness against my wrongdoers made my pain feel real and justified. I felt that if I forgave them I was also somehow excusing the pain they had caused me.

Choosing to receive God's forgiveness in my own life, as well as extending it to others, demanded great courage from me, as it does for many people. When we truly repent and receive God's forgiveness in our life, the slate is washed clean. Likewise, when we forgive those who have sinned against us, we choose to grant them a pardon. We actively declare, "I no longer hold you responsible for the wrong you committed against me." Extending forgiveness can be extremely difficult for a post-abortive woman who has been traumatized and physically violated. If horrific wrongs have been perpetrated against her and her child, she may feel completely justified in holding her wrongdoers responsible for their crimes. She may even believe that her anger towards them strengthens the punishment they should receive.

It was not until I experienced the freedom found in forgiveness that I realized that passing sentence on my accusers was neither my responsibility nor my right; nor was it within my capabilities. That responsibility is in the hands of One far stronger, wiser, and more powerful than we are. If we were truly responsible for the actions of others and the consequences of their actions, the weight of that responsibility would bury us. No matter how deeply affected we might be by another person's choice, we are not responsible for deciding the reward or punishment of their choice. That job belongs to Jesus, and for that I am forever grateful. On the Cross, He took on all the sins of the world. He took on our sin as well as their sin. The weight was lifted off of our shoulders and put onto His. And this knowledge makes me breathe a sigh of relief!

Miraculously, when we choose to forgive others instead of trying to control them, Jesus' light and healing are released to flow within us. I have seen emotional chains, planks, and locked doors fly off post-abortive women when they choose forgiveness. The strong hand of the enemy of our souls, that once had a grasp around that woman, immediately loosens. Even if it takes time, emotional and physical healing will come as a result of forgiving others. When we lead someone into a life of forgiveness, we usher them into freedom from bondage.

Jesus states that living a life of forgiveness is a foundational component in His kingdom. In His famous Sermon on the Mount, He prays, "Our Father in Heaven, . . . forgive us our debts, as we also have forgiven our debtors" (Matthew 6:9–12). This simple prayer, this simple truth, is full of wisdom and power. This is how He instructs us to pray, thus this is how we are instructed to live. We are to forgive our debtors as we have been forgiven.

Then Jesus goes further: "as you forgive others, the Heavenly Father will also forgive you" (Matthew 6:14). In other words, we must forgive others in order to receive the full impact of God's forgiveness in our life. This is completely contrary to how the world and our carnal mind want us to deal with people, but when we walk in forgiveness toward those who have wronged us, we will find that we are released ourselves. We have actually been given the choice, the freedom, to issue our own pardon.

Peter ponders this teaching and follows up with Jesus. "Lord, how often shall my brother sin against me and I forgive him," he asks; "up to seven times?" Jesus replies, "I do not say to you, up to seven times, but up to seventy times seven" (Matthew 18:21–22).

Many post-abortive women have been hurt time and time again. They may have had multiple abortions. They often wonder what Peter did: "Just how many times do I have to forgive? How can I pick myself back up, time and time again? How can I extend mercy over and over when my heart is pierced, my cheek is slapped, and my body is beaten into the ground? How can I live this way?" How *can* they find the courage to forgive multiple times? This is extremely difficult, but Jesus makes very clear the importance of forgiving one another and the severity of the consequences when we don't.

Thankfully, Jesus demonstrated forgiveness in the most powerful way anyone ever has. He was nailed to a cross, took on our shame, and extended His hand of forgiveness even in the midst of excruciating physical and emotional pain. With every blow, insult, and wrongful accusation, He forgave. He walked it out, seventy times seven. Yet He had the power and the right to take matters into His own hands. He could have damned His offenders, but He did not. He forgave them (Luke 23:34). He forgave us and pardoned our insurmountable debt. Now, as His friends, we are given the opportunity to extend the same mercy to others as well as to ourselves. We are not asked to do anything He has not already done.

When God leads us down the path of forgiveness, we come face to face with the wrongs of others as well as our own trespasses. God, in His kindness, leads us into our own moment of repentance. When we get close to Him, His holiness exposes our unrighteousness. He doesn't expose us to condemn us, but to set us free. He broke bread with sinners. He lived among them. Sinners were attracted to Him, because while He was completely truthful, He was also gentle and kind. Although the Pharisees condemned her, Jesus said of Mary of Bethany, "she loves much because she has been forgiven much" (Luke 7:47). Where the Pharisees saw only past mistakes, Jesus saw a heart hungry to know Him. I pray that we can model Jesus to everyone around us.

THE FIVE FORGIVENESS FINGERS

I liken extending and receiving forgiveness after abortion to loosening the grip of a large hand gripping one's throat. The hand's five fingers represent individuals whom it is important for us to forgive. The hand's grip has the power to keep us stationary until we are truly able to forgive ourselves and these individuals. Releasing the grip of each of these five fingers allows us to walk the journey of forgiveness both practically and in complete honesty.

The first finger of the hand has "Him" written on it. "Him" may be a husband, a boyfriend, an acquaintance, or even a family member. In my situation, I was betrayed by my teenage boyfriend. I wondered, "How could a boy lead me into such a mess? How could he lead me to end the life of our child?" I placed all the fault on his head. My anger, and my fear of him, made forgiving him not only seem impossible, but terrifying. It was extremely difficult for me to speak his name out loud or even think about him, much less to go before God with him at the center of our conversation. I had been violated, torn, and left in the dust of his shoes; it took years before this finger completely lost its grip on me. In my mind—and in the minds of many post-abortive women—my anger was justified. It took a restraining order on him for me to legally end our relationship, yet I was still emotionally bound by his control over me for many more months.

This is the case for many women following an abortion or abuse, so we must be extremely sensitive to them. It helps to realize that forgiveness does not mean that a woman has to like "him," have a relationship with him, or even speak of him again. For me, forgiving him meant that I could give my entire relationship with him and all the pain he had caused me to the Lord. I did not have to allow his unfair actions and the memories of them to continue to violently hold me down.

The second finger of the hand represents the doctor and other workers involved in the abortion procedure. In my case, I was mad at them all. The doctor whom I spoke to before my abortion, the nurse who held my hand, the doctor who performed the abortion, the nurse who gave me birth control pills in recovery, and the nurse at the desk who checked me out were all guilty in my mind. I think that just one simple word of comfort or truth from their lips could have changed my decision, but that word was never spoken.

After the abortion, I was left all alone in a room until I was ready to get up and leave— as if I had just had a pedicure. The only contact I had with the abortion clinic workers in recovery was when a nurse came in with birth control pills in her hand and told me I had to take them so I would not go make the same mistake again. After about an hour in recovery, my boyfriend returned from having lunch with a friend, paid Planned Parenthood several hundred dollars, and walked me out without a word from anyone. They had told me before the abortion that they were there to help me, but they weren't. In my view, they were heartless. So I decided they weren't worthy of my forgiveness.

Finally, about two years after my abortion, during a brave moment, I wrote down the name (if I knew it) of each person who had played a part in my abortion process in any way. I wrote down the name of each of these people and, one by one, handed them over to God. I verbally forgave them and I asked the Lord to help me let them go. I focused my prayers specifically on the nurse who, unknowingly, had interrupted a moment of clarity I had had in the clinic, when I had almost decided to run out the door and not come back. This nurse's words persuaded me to go through with my decision to abort, so I was furious at her, and I desperately needed release from my anger. This same practical approach is an excellent way to walk out a process that can seem only theoretical.

Several years later, I worked up the courage to return to that same abortion clinic. This time, I stopped on the sidewalk outside and prayed. I was regularly praying in front of other abortion clinics for the women and workers, and there was a part of me that knew the grip of that finger would be released completely when I stood and prayed in the place of my own haunted past. A friend of mine and I drove over 800 miles, from Georgia to Connecticut, so I could stand strong and face my personal demons. I also needed to completely exonerate the workers in that specific abortion clinic. As I stood there, my hurt miraculously turned into prayer and forgiveness for them.

The third finger represents parents and family members. Many young girls have abortions because their mother takes them to the clinic or threatens to kick them out of the house if they don't have the abortion. While standing in front of abortion clinics on a publicly proclaimed "Abortion Day," I have seen mothers almost drag their noticeably pregnant teenage daughters through the clinic door. I believe that many of these young girls don't want to have an abortion, but they see no other option. Such emotional pressure leads to a collection of hurts that can lead to broken family relationships for years to come.

Even if a woman's parents didn't know about the abortion or are not repentant themselves, it's still crucial to address this area of forgiveness. Perhaps some women feel they can't trust their parents enough to disclose their situation to them or that sharing would still not result in their parents' support. My parents didn't learn of my abortion until several years after my decision, but there still were times when I held them responsible for it. I think I was just trying to find someone else to blame and they were an easy target, but I needed to forgive them.

Depending on the circumstance and a woman's relationship with her parents, it may not be beneficial for a woman to forgive her parents in person. For one reason, her parents may not actually be at fault at all. It is best to ask God for the appropriate way to walk out this part of the journey. For me, I felt it was important that I tell my parents about the abortion rather than keep it a secret. For some women, though, it might be just as helpful to write their family members a letter of forgiveness, whether they ever actually send the letter to them or not.

The fourth finger represents forgiving yourself. This finger is the one most likely to hold a woman the tightest. God wants every post-abortive woman to be able to stand in a mirror and see herself the way He sees her: as a beloved daughter who made a terrible mistake. God is the lifter-up of our head, and despite whatever mistakes are in our past, He wants us to be able to hold our heads up high because we know our identity in Him. For many women after an abortion, though, this seems like an unreachable reality. Post-abortive women may see themselves as filthy, covered in mud and ashes, for years after the abortion.

The trauma a woman endures as a result of an abortion can completely wreck everything she believes about herself. Labels, secrets, and lies have to be demolished and replaced with reality and truth. For this rebuilding process to be successful, a post-abortive woman requires help from the community around her. God is powerful and more than able, but He also gave us each other to be His hands and feet in our lives. The lies are so strong that we need to hear the truth from someone else.

The last finger of forgiveness represents God. No, of course God doesn't actually need to be forgiven. He is completely holy, righteous, and pure. But we don't always see Him rightly. We are broken people who often have a broken image of God. We too often don't believe He is really who He says He is. We often don't understand why something happened the way that it did, why He allowed it to happen, or where He was in the midst of our pain. Those are very real emotions and questions that need to be resolved in the hearts of many women after an abortion. Thankfully, God isn't offended by our unrighteous anger towards Him. He isn't scared when we doubt or question Him. He desires to reveal Himself to us, give us clarity, and embrace our heart with the truth—even when we wrongly believe that He is the one who caused our pain.

It is important for all of us, including all post-abortive women, to come before God honestly. Many times we hold on to disillusionment with God only because we aren't fully honest about the way that we feel about Him. It's normal to wonder where He was, why He didn't intervene, and why He allowed us to go through with the pain that we did. But we gain incredible clarity when we get close enough to Him to be honest with Him. God isn't offended by our honesty. We can approach His throne of grace with confidence rather than fear (Hebrews 4:16). So when we minister to others who are angry at God, we mustn't become offended by their view of God or their anger towards Him.

I pray that as women get close to God, He will encounter them with His love and show them where He was before, during, and after their abortion. When I have led women into this healing encounter, I encourage them to close their eyes and ask God to show them where He was in their moment of pain. I pray that their eyes will be opened to see and their ears will be opened to hear His response. I lead them through a series of questions to ask God, and then we simply wait for Him to answer. Where was He when she found out she was pregnant? Where was He when she was driving to the abortion clinic? Where was He in the clinic? Where was He in the abortion room? Where was He in the recovery room? Where was He in her house when she got home? Where is He now? What expression does He have on His face?

In order for a ministry time like this to be powerful and real, we must believe that God speaks to us and desires to encounter us. We must believe that He desires to open our eyes and show us who He is and where He is. He is real, alive, and near. Many post-abortive women desperately need believers to lead them into these truths. God is nearer than we usually think.

These questions, of course, can be prayed through alone without someone else, but it is even more powerful when we minister to one another and agree in prayer. God can take these painful moments and bring comfort through His embrace. If a woman did not feel His presence in the midst of the painful moments of the past, perhaps as she goes through these questions and a time of prayer, she will feel Him in the present. It could also be beneficial to write each question down and then find a corresponding scripture about God's nearness and love that reveals the answer.

Freedom and forgiveness are available to everyone—even the person who commits the supposed "unforgiveable" sin.

God wants to loosen the grip of this tight-fisted hand that is squeezing the life out of millions of women across our country. So many women have tried desperately to move on from their abortion and to forgive their accusers but have found this to be an impossible task. The 'A' branded on their soul prevents them from experiencing true forgiveness and freedom. I thought that choosing abortion would allow me to move on with my life, when in fact it only caused me to lose all hope and the ability to dream big dreams for my life. It was only when I was able to overcome the lies I believed about myself and forgive the other people involved that I was able to move forward.

When I think about the years I walked through my healing journey with the Lord, I'm reminded of the story of the Samaritan woman at the well (John 4:7-29). Jesus went to meet this woman at a well where many people gathered frequently for water. He deliberately went out of His way to meet this specific woman at this particular well. In His determination to reach out to her, Jesus crossed racial and cultural lines. He already knew everything she had done, as well as the sin that consumed her present. But neither her past nor her present swayed Him. He did not condemn her, yell at her, or point out her flaws. Rather, He revealed to her who He was for her.

This woman realized that Jesus had been with her through all her sin and suffering. In the holy moments and the sinful moments, He was there, pursuing her. I can imagine there must have been moments in her past when she had imagined God looking upon her with disappointment and shame. When she gave in to temptation she likely imagined His face burning with anger against her. She had constructed a false image of God in her mind. Yet in that moment, as Jesus stood before her, He was smiling at her. Jesus exposed her secrets, true. But as terrifying as that can be, He did it out of a deep love for her; the deepest love.

A woman who probably had kept to herself in shame, clinging to her secret life—or not so secret—was soon running through the streets proclaiming truth. The Bible tells us, "The woman left her water pot and went into the city and said to the men: 'Come, see a man who told me all the things that I have done'" (John 4:27–29). She was changed forever. Could she change the past? Of course not, but now she was able to see that God could change her future.

Sadly, we can never bring back the children who have been lost to abortion. Nevertheless, freedom and forgiveness are available to everyone—even the person who commits the supposed "unforgiveable" sin. True freedom looks like the Samaritan woman joyfully running through the streets after her encounter with Jesus. We may not see a woman run through the streets, but we can all believe for millions of men and women, new creations in God, once again running after their dreams and into the arms of Jesus.

Chapter Seven

HEALING BOTH INSIDE AND OUT

Oh Lord my God, I cried to You for Help, and You healed me.

Psalm 30:2

JESUS IS ENCOUNTERING THE POST-ABORTIVE women in America. Women who have experienced devastating trauma emotionally, physically, and relationally are putting on their running shoes, so to speak. This is thrilling! I celebrate the miraculous emotional freedom taking place, and I believe that much of it is due to the Church stepping up the plate.

Yet dare we not believe for more miracles? I believe that God has even more in store for the walking wounded post-abortive women among us, as well as those who have already found a sense of freedom. Despite the emotional miracles taking place, many of these courageous women are still bound by physical or relational consequences from their choices made five, fifteen, or even thirty years ago. The recovery books, retreats, and counseling often stop short of helping these women achieve complete wholeness. Yes, there are consequences to sin, yet because of God's grace I know that a woman's physical and relational needs are also within His healing reach.

It is time to call forth women who are suffering from physical trauma into a deeper level of faith in God as their healer. It is time that we pray, believe, and step out of our self-erected comfort zones and begin to function in the authority given to us by Jesus. Unbelief and fear have crippled our impact in the lives of women, as well as others God brings through our doors. God is our great physician. He longs to heal people, and He wants to heal through the hands of you and me. He is the great I Am. Women repeatedly suffer from miscarriages, infertility, and even breast cancer following abortions. These terrible things are common life events in the lives of women all around us. Will you believe with me that the post-abortive women in our lives can walk free of these burdens?

For years, I have stood alongside women who were standing behind the popular post-abortion sign that reads, "I Regret My Abortion." I have great respect for these women, many of whom are dear friends of mine, yet there is much more available in God for women than a life of regret. Wholeness is available for each miraculous beauty behind that sign, whether the need is restoration in a suffering marriage or physical healing from infertility. All her needs are interrelated, and all deserve equal attention. The Holy Spirit sees all needs, and when He is free to move, miraculous breakthrough follows. A dam breaks and suddenly emotional breakthrough can become the answer to a physical breakthrough. The Scriptures tell us that Jesus taught in the synagogues, proclaimed the good news, and healed "every disease and sickness among the people" (Matthew 4:23). Just one touch of His garment resulted in supernatural deliverance.

What would it look like for us to have the faith and determination to press through the crowd, leading by the hand a physically damaged post-abortive woman to the hem of His garment? The Church is supposed to be a light on a hill. We are those whom the broken people should run to, believing that a touch or a word can change their lives. Instead, the statistics show that our fear, busyness, and apathy may have contributed to thousands of abortions. Let us not be like the Pharisees who were more concerned about the Sabbath-day laws and rituals than they were in seeing a man healed and a life changed.

> God is our great physician. He longs to heal people, and He wants to heal through the hands of you and me.

Just as the first disciples were, we too have been commissioned to proclaim the gospel, heal the sick, cast out demons, and raise the dead. That is a serious commission, and a command that has not been retracted since the day it left the lips of Jesus. When we ask, He hears from heaven. What is keeping us from tapping into the remarkable Christian life available to us in God? We too often shrink back in fear and unbelief that our prayers will not be answered.

I understand how difficult it can be for someone to have hope for healing. It can be heart-wrenching for a desperate woman to believe that God will heal her womb after an abortion and bring life where barrenness has prevailed. But we must stand on the Scriptures and believe that God is who He says He is. For too long we have relied primarily on medical institutions or medications to redeem our lives (or to merely put a Band-Aid over painful symptoms). I thank God for medicine and medical expertise, but have we forgotten our great Physician? He created the universe and all the systems in it, and He is still alive and active in our world today.

HEALING INSIDE AND OUT

The physical risks following abortion are tremendous, yet we rarely read the warning labels. They remain locked in darkness as the mainstream media parades the "heroic" efforts of Planned Parenthood. Yet an abortion not only snuffs out a life within a mother's womb, it also greatly increases the risk that the mother will experience trauma to her womb that could affect her future physically in many ways. We cannot neglect these facts before considering an abortion, nor can we neglect them when ministering to a woman after an abortion. Research and common sense tell us that trauma to the woman's uterus can cause *postpartum* hemorrhage, future miscarriages, and even infertility. Unfortunately, "although uterine perforation with intra-abdominal injury is a well-described complication of vacuum aspiration termination of pregnancy, most post-abortion perforations go undetected."[26] So the majority of women suffering from uterine perforation don't even know to seek medical attention. In addition to these risks, there is the risk of the woman developing severe *postpartum* depression,[27] breast cancer,[28]

---

26   Elizabeth Ring and Cassidy Ian Gentles, *Women's Health after Abortion: The Medical and Psychological Evidence*, 2nd ed. (Toronto: DeVeber Institute for Bioethics and Social Research, 2003), 71.

27   J.R. Cougle, D.C. Reardon, and P.K. Coleman, "Depression Associated with Abortion and Childbirth: A Long-Term Analysis of the NLSY Cohort," *Medical Science Monitor* 9(4): CR105-112, 2003.

28   Ring and Gentles, *Women's Health*, 28.

and even death.[29] These risks are already high after just one abortion, and they only increase with every subsequent abortion.[30]

Unfortunately, about half of the post-abortive women in the United States have had or will have multiple abortions.[31] Many women have used abortion as a form of birth control, neglecting the fact that their need for control over their uterus may actually lead to a damaged uterus unable to nurture children they hoped to have in the future. These risks are extremely serious and common, yet women are exposed to them time and time again, and usually without their knowledge. Risks naturally increase when we interrupt God's design and interfere harshly with the natural processes a woman's body needs to go through when she conceives a child. Thankfully, God is merciful, and He loves to heal the physical complications that result from an abortion just as much as He loves to heal the emotional scars. In the name of "hope" and "choice," the abortion industry and our American medical institutions are treating women and their bodies with horrible indifference and abuse. As a childbirth educator and labor coach, I work with women every day who have been traumatized in these ways. I see the emotional pain that is caused in a woman when her body has been hijacked and its natural ability underestimated and violated. The emotional pain can be devastating and the physical damages severe and permanent. We too often forget that God created women and the blessings He put inside of them. We should show them the respect and honor they deserve.

---

29   David C. Reardon *et al*, "Deaths Associated with Pregnancy Outcome: A Record Linkage Study of Low-Income Women. Elliot Institute," *Southern Medical Journal*, vol. 95/8, August 2002.
30   *Women's Health*, 100.
31   Ibid.

The abortion debate is not an issue of choice; it is a human rights issue for both the unborn child as well as the mother. The tide has to turn, and it begins with us respecting those whom God gives us to minister to. We must act and pray in boldness to change the culture of death around us instead of simply sitting on our hands in indifference, fear, and defeat. The lives of women and children are in danger.

ABORTION & MARRIAGE

As we consider the physical effects of abortion, we must also consider the relational consequences of abortion. Sin has consequences. These consequences naturally spill into our relationships. "One study found that of the more than 400 couples who went through the abortion experience, 70% of the relationships failed within one month after the abortion."[32] Even for married couples, an abortion during the marriage has the potential to completely devastate the relationship. Contrary to popular belief, divorce rates are steadily decreasing.[33] God is on the move in marriages, but marriages that experience abortion are at a much greater risk of brokenness and divorce. It is truly wonderful that the divorce rate is decreasing, but we should hope for more in marriage than merely surviving and escaping divorce by the skin of our teeth. Let's fight for fulfilling and exhilarating marriages that consistently reflect the nature of God. Many marriages in the church are currently in ruins from abortions still hidden in secret or abortions committed openly without healing and reconciliation.

---

32   Nancy Michels, *Helping Women Recover from Abortion* (Minneapolis, MN: Bethany House, 1988), 159.

33   "National Marriage and Divorce Rate Trends," Centers for Disease Control and Prevention, http://www.cdc.gov/nchs/nvss/marriage_divorce_tables.htm/.

A godly marriage declares the glory of God to the culture around us. It declares who God is as our Bridegroom and we as His bride. But our culture is continually pushing the cultural standard further from God's ordained one. Because of the impact for the kingdom of God that a godly marriage can make on a nation's culture, I believe this push against righteousness will continue. The enemy will do anything he can do to steal, kill, and destroy a godly marriage. Abortion is one of these devastating attempts. When an abortion takes place within a marriage covenant or before a covenant is made, it releases distrust, shame, and darkness into a sacred space. Losing a child is already one of the most painful life experiences any couple could experience. When that life is taken by the hand of one or both parties in a marriage, this massively compounds the grief and pain.

God wants to repair the broken pieces of our lives and give us marriages of power. If abortion has been introduced into a marriage, we have to bring that darkness into the light and slowly build back the pieces. We can never expect a couple to simply "move on" or "just work it out." Abortion must be taken very seriously, whether it occurs within the marriage or is brought into a marriage. Even when the woman herself has worked through her past and has been reconciled with the Lord, we cannot simply assume that her soon-to-be husband or current husband has been as well. Peace must be found by all.

Thankfully, following my abortion, I walked a miraculous healing journey before I was married. Because of my ministry in the pro-life arena, my husband already knew of my abortion before we started dating. Yet when we married, we realized that my decision did not only affect me: it affected our entire family. Realizing that he could have been my child's father caused my husband to mourn deeply over my unborn child's fate. He took practical steps to honor her as his own child, and we grieved her together. Because of our honesty and intentionality, we are now able to celebrate our child's life together, and one day, when they are old enough to understand, we will be able to welcome our other children into our journey as well.

A decision I made sixteen years ago will affect our family for years to come. We all lost a loved one, and we intend on recognizing this rather than hiding it away as a family secret. I realize that not every marriage will walk the same journey as my husband and I did, yet every couple that has experienced abortion must recognize the emotional healing that needs to take place. Finding their own path to healing will take wisdom, comfort, and assistance from the community around them.

God wants to heal marriages. He takes the marriage covenant very seriously, and He longs for us to live out His wonderful intentions in our marriage relationships. We can trust Him for His best for us.

REPLACEMENT BABY

The grief and loss experienced by parents from losing a child is almost beyond the imagination. We all can appreciate the long road of healing and recovery any parent would have to walk after losing a child. We can recognize their need for help, community, and prayer. We can understand the need for time to process, grieve, and mourn the loss of their baby. Though we might not have the words to comfort them, we can all appreciate the pain that these parents endure and may hold on to for the rest of their lives.

It can be difficult, though, to appreciate the mourning a parent goes through after losing a child whom they *never met*. Because the parents (and we) never held their baby in their arms, we (and they) might not understand that this same grief is present. Many mothers and fathers, not surprisingly, suppress their grief. Also, our society has deeply ingrained in many people's minds that that unborn baby was not really a baby. Yet even in cases when the parent or parents are content with their abortion choice, deep grief will often surface months or even years down the road. Emotional triggers such as marriage, the loss of a loved one, or a future pregnancy can remove an applied emotional "band-aid" from the unrecognized wound.

Even though I made my abortion choice sixteen years ago, not a day goes by that I do not think about my child. I carry her with me in my heart. She was inside of me, though she was so small. I was her mother and I always will be. I am not in despair over her lost life any more, and now I can even rejoice over her. But it took several years for me to resolve in my heart that I did not have to "just move on" and forget someone whom I loved, and love, so deeply. I will never simply "move on" or forget about her. Why would I ever want to?

Yes, there is a natural grieving process after the loss of a child. And God does want us all to be emotionally healthy and happy. But would we ever suggest to a mother who has recently lost a child that she should find the strength to *forget* about her child? Of course we wouldn't. But women who have had abortions hear this suggestion frequently. As a result, they tend to adapt—as best they can—to their sorrow and to hide from their emotions. Their tears are reserved for their lonely bedrooms so that others (not they themselves) can "move on." And of course the abortion industry is built upon the lie that her child was never really a person anyway, so the mother might try to convince herself that this is the truth simply to be able to find an ounce of freedom from her mourning.

Many women, not surprisingly (and especially so when the grieving process is suppressed), end up trying to fill their empty arms with another child. This might mean that a woman will intentionally get pregnant to literally replace the baby, or that she views her next pregnancy, even years down the road, as a longed-for replacement for the child she aborted. In post-abortion recovery counseling this is referred to as "desiring a replacement baby." Despite our society's telling them to "move on" from one baby they lost, many women believe that healing will come only from having another one. (This is also often the case with women who have suffered a miscarriage.)

The Lord can and sometimes does bring healing after the birth of another child, but He doesn't bless someone with another child merely in an effort to replace the aborted baby. It is extremely important that we acknowledge and individually embrace each life entrusted to us. Trying to replace one baby with another is damaging to the mother as well as the child. Typically, the healing that she thought would come at the birth of her baby only worsens. Gazing at her long-awaited baby's tiny toes and fingers can actually be debilitating, because she's reminded of her earlier loss. When a known "replacement baby" is welcomed into a home, it is extremely important for both the mother and father to seek counseling and prayer. In those cases when the mother's emotional healing doesn't take place until after the replacement child is already older, it may also be appropriate to seek that child's forgiveness or seek counseling for them.

Personally, I was able to avoid the need for a replacement baby by fully acknowledging and embracing my unborn child for who she was and who she could have become. I began by rejecting people's disingenuous suggestions that I should forget about my aborted daughter. Rather than forgetting her, I spent hours before the Lord asking Him for His heart for my child. God then led me to have a memorial service for my baby, to honor her life. The service was a beautiful celebration of the short life she lived in my womb, and one of the most powerful days of my life. My daughter, Hannah, is honored at the National Memorial for the Unborn in Chattanooga, Tennessee, which is where we held the memorial service. My family and friends attended, and the service was videotaped for my (then future) husband and children. I was given a certificate of life with Hannah's name on it that I will forever cherish.

Acknowledging and honoring my baby in this way, openly admitting that she is gone and can never be replaced, not only helped me embrace her life, it helped bring closure to my heart. It was also important to me to declare publicly that my daughter existed and that she mattered. My daughter's life was a precious gift to me, as are the lives of my other children. I only wish I could have understood that when she was still with me. Delivering my three other children has been a continuation of healing and freedom for me, as I have experienced the gift of motherhood that the Lord always desired to give me. Taking the time to fully grieve the loss of my first baby, though, has led to a greater amount of freedom and ability to truly love each one of my children for who they are, without carrying previous pain and loss into our relationship.

Although I was extremely intentional about not carrying the pain of my loss into my relationships with my future children, not every post-abortive woman is that intentional, or even knows to be or how to be. This is another way that we can help these women. At my daughter's memorial service, I was approached by the director of the National Memorial for the Unborn. I will never forget her encouragement to me. She said, "Cathy, I believe the service you just had and the honor you gave your baby will be contagious. I pray that many more services just like yours will take place here." I hope she is right. Not every woman is emotionally ready to have a memorial service like that, nor is it the healing path for every post-abortive woman. We must encourage and support the post-abortive women we know, though, and provide a safe space for them to grieve where they won't feel condemned or ridiculed. Giving them a place to grieve for as long as they need it, and sharing their tears with them, can change not only their life but the lives of their entire family.

INFERTILITY

Infertility and miscarriage are both common consequences of one or more abortions. Despite this tragic reality, God's word assures us that He is the maker of all things. He is the one who has the power and authority to open and close the womb. We live in a fallen world where sin abounds, and there are real consequences to sin. On this side of Heaven, God's people experience pain, disease, and even death. We must remember, though, that "where sin abounds, grace abounds all the more" (Romans 5:20). Whether a woman's barrenness is due to an abortion, birth control, or for unknown reasons, God wants to heal the wombs of women, and He wants the church to pray and believe that He can do it.

God commanded Adam and Eve to be fruitful and multiply. Yet the Bible records that Sarah and Hannah experienced the pain of barrenness, just as many women do today. Amazingly though, these two women also experienced monumental promises. Barren or not, God's promises to us are always "Yes" and "Amen." His promises are meant to be believed, fought for, and held on to.

The prayer to bear a child in our womb goes far beyond just us as an individual or a couple. Our prayer is also about praying for God's promises to come to pass over us, our family, and even our nation. God desires to raise up godly children from our wombs who will shake the earth with humility, righteousness, and justice. I believe that the time will come when we will say over hundreds of women, "Blessed are the childless women, the wombs that never bore and the breasts that never nursed" (Luke 23:29).

Sometimes we have to just go ahead and thank God for what He is going to do, in spite of any doubt we might feel. The more we walk in thankfulness, the more our heart will catch up to our spirit and will be filled with hope rather than despair. We must have the audacity to declare the promises of God into being. Does the Church of America have the audacity to believe God? Would you dare to believe with the women around you for complete healing of their wombs and hearts after an abortion?

The Man who healed the woman with the issue of blood (Luke 8:43–48) is the same Man who is alive today. He still has the same desire burning in His heart to heal women in desperate need of His power. What set that woman apart from many others was not only her faith to believe for healing, but also her determination to *declare* and *claim* her healing. It takes great courage to believe like this. I have known multiple women who have prayed for years for the healing of their womb. Tears have flowed from my own eyes over promises to them that a child would come . . . and I have seen these promises fulfilled time and time again. I believe that God is looking for women who will look upon the injustice that has been done them and their child, and yet celebrate in anticipation of His ultimate victory.

> The post-abortive women in our nation need much more than merely a nice pat on the head. They need men and women of miraculous power and faith to reach out and say, "Be healed, in the mighty name of Jesus."

As women all across our nation come forth in bravery to touch the hem of His garment, I pray that their weeping will cease, because He is good and His mercies endure forever. The post-abortive women in our nation need much more than merely a nice pat on the head. They need men and women of miraculous power and faith to reach out and say, "Be healed, in the mighty name of Jesus." You may not have silver or gold, but you do have Jesus (Acts 3:6). And Jesus is always enough. True redemption for every post-abortive woman, every family, and every community comes only when we can turn to the Lord, not only as the One who died on the Cross for our sins, but also as the One who rose from the dead to give us life. This is the gospel of Jesus Christ. He is alive, not dead, and He is here in our midst. Guilt, anger, shame, and infertility after abortion must bow their knee to this Man.

Chapter Eight

THE ONLY TRUE SOLUTION

You can never learn that Christ is all you need, until Christ is all you have.

—Corrie ten Boom

IF WE WALK IN BOLDNESS and make ourselves available, we may all find ourselves face-to-face with a woman in need. There will be times when we know how to help, and there will likely be many more when we do not. It can be difficult to find words that will genuinely express compassion. It can be challenging to find the practical means that will bring peace and support. When we minister to those in deep pain and anguish, hard questions will surely arise. Many of these questions will take us by surprise or leave us short of words. For years, I walked the road to healing with a compassionate community of believers around me. Some knew how to help, but many more did not. I read book after book on how to find healing after abortion, yet still I was left with emotional pain. The community, the practical help, and the Bible studies were helpful and necessary, but in the end there was only one solution to my emotional turmoil: His name is Jesus.

Jesus revealed facets of His character to me that enlightened my eyes and ushered me into true peace. He ministered to the unreached places of my heart that no book or friend could reach. I searched Jesus out not only as my Savior but also as my Judge, my Prince of Peace, and my Bridegroom. In His courtroom my anger dissolved, the guilt and shame resting on my shoulders fell at the feet of my Prince of Peace, and I found my home in Him as my Bridegroom. There are many helpful and needed steps we can and should take to help someone following an abortion, but ultimately only one gift will remain, and that is Jesus. Compared to the deep healing work He can do, our best efforts and wisest words are meaningless and will one day fade away. Jesus is the greatest gift we can offer.

GIVING YOUR ANGER TO THE JUDGE

The nearness of Jesus is sweet and it is tender. Yet just as He is tender, He is also jealous, holy, and righteousness. He is all of Himself, all the time. During my post-abortion recovery, Jesus gave me a simple yet profound revelation, one that no one in any church had revealed to me. It is this: Jesus is our great Judge. In His tenderness, He sits on the throne. In His nearness, He holds the government on His shoulders. In His kindness, He brings forth judgments and extends His hand of mercy.

> Jesus is powerful and all-knowing, yet His hand is always open. His gaze is always tender. His words are seasoned with grace. He is the approachable Judge.

This revelation is not only one of the most wonderful I

have ever uncovered about Jesus, but it came in the time of my greatest need. The truth hit me: Jesus is not only the Judge of the earth, but He is also my personal judge. We will not only stand before Him face-to-face at the end of our days, but He is near to us in our day to day. He judges, He refines, and He corrects, but He is also our defender, who sees and hears our side of the story. Jesus is unlike any other judge we will ever encounter. He is unlike the judge we see in the movies or in the up-and-coming television show. He is unlike the judges sitting in courtrooms across our land. His Court is higher than the Supreme Court. Though the impact of a Supreme Court ruling is grand and sweeping, Jesus has the final say. This realization is altogether terrifying, yet also comforting for one who has been wronged by the abortion industry, has lost a child at the hands of deception and fear, and who now prays for the ending of one of the greatest wars of our time: the war against children and motherhood. The justified anger that I carried for so many years, against those who had committed such terrible crimes against me and my baby, sounded absurd when I considered His authority.

With fire in His eyes and unwavering determination in His heart, Jesus makes every judgment out of total love. He is the jealous lover sitting on the judgment seat. His judgments, whether obviously merciful or an overt act of punishment, are all done out of His mercy. He always wants to bring His people into a greater love and to bring unbelievers into His kingdom. He is powerful and all-knowing, yet His hand is always open. His gaze is always tender. His words are seasoned with grace. He is the approachable Judge. He is not far off. Many of us only view Him as looming over us, the Judge who punishes every wrong move. We wait in fear for the resounding sound of

His gavel. Yet do we also see Him as the Judge who defends and protects those whom He loves? That was one truth I had not considered.

An earthly judge is someone who has been given authority to hear and decide cases in a court of law. They administer justice in a situation. A judge's role is to hear all sides of the case and then to make an authoritative decision that will settle the case for all parties. We need judges in our society to administer justice where there has been abuse of the law and someone's rights have been infringed upon. Because of the power and authority they wield, a judge can be intimidating to the average citizen. In the midst of the ordered chaos of a courtroom, a petitioner might wonder if the judge truly heard their case. Both parties in a trial hope that they presented their case well enough so that the punishment will fall on the other party. This becomes even more complicated when the judge is seen to be unjust. Many post-abortive women feel that they live in an unjust judge's courtroom. They feel that their case has never truly been heard and justly settled; therefore, anger swells in their hearts.

Jesus told a story about a widow who sought justice from an unjust judge. We are told that this woman's judge did not fear God nor did he respect man. Nevertheless, "she kept coming to him, saying 'Give me legal protection from my opponent'" (Luke 18:2-5). The woman was persistent. She was not intimidated by this judge's personality or reputation. And eventually her persistence and courage paid off and the judge granted her legal protection. This woman had been wronged, just as many women in our nation have been wronged. As a widow and as a woman, the cards were stacked against her. Nonetheless, she remained persistent. Even though she knew that she stood before an unjust judge, she kept coming. Jesus concluded,

"Hear what the unrighteous judge said. Now will not God bring about justice for His elect who cry to Him day and night, and will He delay long over them? I tell you that He will bring about justice for them quickly" (Luke 18:6–8).

Will Jesus, your Judge, bring about justice on your behalf when you cry out to Him? Yes, the Scriptures say that it is so. The key is crying out to Him and believing Him for it. God sees those who are far off, but for those who draw near, He listens and He acts. Just as in the story of this brave and persistent widow, God hears the post-abortive woman. When no one else has listened or has really understood her, He does. When this woman feels like a widow, abandoned by a loved one, forgotten, God has His eye on her.

Many women have been abused, neglected, and forgotten, or they feel as if they have been. Jesus, the Judge, cares about them deeply though, and He hears their case in the courts of Heaven. It is not all right with Him that a woman and her baby have been stripped of their dignity and robbed of the chance of life. When a post-abortive woman truly believes this revelation, her anger can fade before His throne of righteousness. Psalm 68:5 says that He is "a father to the fatherless and a judge for the widows." He makes all things new and defends those who are overlooked or forgotten. The author of Lamentations cries out, "O Lord, you have seen my oppression; judge my case" (Lamentations 3:59). Millions of women around the world are crying out this prayer.

When I realized Jesus' jealousy for me as my personal judge, it turned my anger towards those who had wronged me into prayers for them. I felt His jealousy burn for me, and it led me to pray for mercy rather than wrath for those who had sinned against me. He allowed me to get just close enough to feel the warmth radiating from His flames. I felt His love burning for me as a loving earthly father's would for His abused daughter. Many women believe that God's anger burns against them, when in fact what they are feeling is His jealousy for them. When we realize this, we can walk into His courtroom with confidence that He will hear our every word. He will tenderly handle our case.

> Many women have been abused, neglected, and forgotten, or they feel as if they have been.

There will be times when our memories try to haunt us or those past hurts try to convince us that we are unworthy of love, but the revelation of Jesus as our Judge reminds us not only of His forgiveness, but also of His jealousy for justice and righteousness. He is jealous to bring truth, show mercy, and bring us deeper into love and holiness. His jealousy is dangerously fierce; waters cannot quench its flame. As a woman who had been deeply hurt, I desperately needed to know this fierce love that will make all wrong things right again. Jesus sees the wrongs done to women and babies by the abortion industry, and His jealousy burns for them. They need to feel the warmth from those flames. In the heat of that flame we are refined and purified, but we are also defended and avenged.

GIVING YOUR GUILT AND SHAME TO THE PRINCE OF PEACE

Living a Cinderella lie, as so many post-abortive women do, becomes exhausting. Trying to appear royal, when beneath our skin we know we are just a simple peasant girl, quickly loses its luster. Shame and guilt tap women on their shoulders, reminding them of what they have done and who they will surely become. Constantly they shout, "Give up!" in her ears. Guilt points out that scarlet letter sewn to the sleeve of her dress. Many post-abortive women only dream of waltzing around the ballroom of life, living full of hope and dreams like everyone else around them. Unfortunately, when they awaken from that dream, they still see the devastation that remains in their heart. Like Cinderella, many women are tempted to run from every romantic relationship so that their "true self" won't be revealed.

Most of us can relate to such feelings. Guilt and shame tell us some of the most powerful lies we could ever believe. They have a sly and sneaky way of slithering into every relationship and every dream. They tell us that our identity is wrapped up by, twisted up in, and covered up by what we have done. This was my story. I was a maiden walking around wishing to be royal but thinking that I never could be, because I felt as if there were a huge "Abortion!" label strapped to me. Even after I was set free from the guilt and shame surrounding my abortion, I still caught myself taking on "Post-Abortive Woman" as my identity. The most difficult times were when someone asked me (before I had my other children) if I had children. What was I supposed to say? To my conversationalist it sounded like an easy get-to-know-you question, but for a very long time it was devastatingly personal to me. A simple conversation told me that instead of wearing a crown of glory as the Bible says, I wore a wig of guilt. The truth is, I have had an abortion. I am a mother, and I have a baby resting with Jesus until I meet her. This is a truth that I cannot change. I cannot take it back, and my baby will always be a part of who I am. But even though I made a terrible choice and I miss my baby terribly, I am still Cathy. I am still me, the me that God created in His perfect image.

When we find ourselves in moments of despair, our greatest tool is the Word of God. If you are mentoring or walking with someone who has had an abortion, one of the greatest gifts you can give them is the Bible. The Word of God is living and active and sharper than a double-edged sword. It is sharp enough to cut those annoying companions of guilt and shame off her shoulders and put them under her feet where they belong. No matter how much we try to help, no matter how often we lend a shoulder to cry on, we cannot provide the peace, security, and unconditional love that we find in God's written Word.

Paul describes in Ephesians the armor that we are offered through the Word. This armor is a set of new clothes for all of us. For a woman who has had an abortion, buying this set of new clothes is the best shopping trip you could ever take her on. Every morning when she looks in the mirror they will remind her of the truth. She is welcomed to strap the breastplate of righteousness across her chest and wear it like a badge. The blood of Jesus washes the scarlet letter off of her dress. She can hold up her shield of faith in front of her when the enemy tries to hit her with his fiery darts of lies. She can put on the helmet of salvation and wear it confidently, like a fancy-hat lady would wear: a big, gaudy hat, full of feathers. In Jesus, her destiny is life. This is something to be excited about. Because of the armor given to her in Christ, a woman who was once gripped by fear can now wear fancy slippers of peace and waltz around the dance floor with Jesus, her Prince of Peace.

The Word of God is our most powerful tool. It is alive, and it became flesh. His name is Jesus, and He is our Prince of Peace. When the Word truly comes alive in our hearts, the woman hiding in the attic like Cinderella can come down, put on her wedding dress, and walk down the aisle to meet her prince. You might say that this story is just a silly cartoon, but I know, because I experienced it, that this is the destiny of millions of women in our nation and around the world. They need to know that, in Christ, they are royalty, not filthy rags. Jesus is truly their Prince. He brings peace to their storm. Only He truly knows them, what they have done, and where they have come from. And His affections are sincere. He is truly a place of peace and refuge.

Just as the prophet Isaiah foretold, a child was born to us, a son was given to us, the government will rest on His shoulders, and His name will be called Wonderful Counselor, Mighty God, Eternal Father, and Prince of Peace (Isaiah 9:6). He knows it all, He is over it all, He is in control, and even in the midst of our confusion and chaos, He is faithful to pursue as our Prince. His pursuit of every post-abortive woman is unfailing and passionate. When my eyes were opened to know His passionate pursuit, I found His peaceful love notes everywhere. They were taped to every mirror where my eyes caught a glimpse of my reflection, they were at my bedside table when I awoke in terror from another dream of my abortion, and they were written on my hand as I stretched it out to introduce myself in a new relationship. His peace began to pursue me around every wrong turn and at every roadblock. Slowly but surely, I found a peace in Him that no one else could offer. The peace I found is available to every post-abortive woman.

FINDING ACCEPTANCE IN THE BRIDEGROOM

Jesus is our safe place. He is our home. His name, Prince of Peace, suggests an element of belonging and even of romance. He is the one who saves the day and who knows all the answers. When we don't have the words to offer a post-abortive woman or man in despair, Jesus always gets the last word. What does it feel like to not only have peace in our minds and hearts but to actually be romanced by peace? This is what His name suggests. He pursues us with peace. Can you imagine what that would feel like to a woman who has lost all peace? What does it feel like to be pursued by peace, led by peace, and embraced by peace? Jesus is peace itself. When we call Him our Prince of Peace, we are saying that He will pursue us in His peace. He leads us by His peace. He wraps us inside His peace. He becomes our peace. Jesus and I are made one, and thus peace engulfs me. I long to live in this reality every day of my life. No matter what happens to me or what circumstance I find myself in, peace is my portion. This is a supernatural way of living.

The idea of being pursued by God with a romantic and jealous love is a foreign idea to many of us. If it is to you or someone you are ministering to, I understand. My life took a 180-degree turn—maybe even a 360—when I realized that Jesus truly does loves me. I'm talking about more than merely the children's song. I mean that He really loves me. He adores me. He pursues me. He is after me like a jealous lover, just waiting to sweep me off my feet every day. Yes, I said it. Jesus is our lover. He is our Bridegroom. He is the Prince every heart longs to be with. Even when this concept of Jesus as my Bridegroom was foreign to my mind, my soul resounded, "Please let it be so!" After all, that is what we were all created for.

Reading the Song of Solomon is one of the most tangible ways by which we can get to know our Bridegroom Jesus. In this book we read of a king who pursues an ordinary woman who becomes extraordinary because of his embrace and acceptance. She finds her true home, and this home is better than she could have ever asked for or imagined. Also, in Ephesians chapter 3, Paul prays for the Ephesians, "that Christ may dwell in your hearts through faith; and that you, being rooted and grounded in love, may be able to comprehend with all the saints what is the breadth and length and height and depth, and to know the love of Christ which surpasses knowledge, that you may be filled up to all the fullness of God" (Ephesians 3:17–19). The love of Christ is beyond our comprehension, yet He desires for us to know His love, to the extent that our weak earthly frames can bear it.

Our Heavenly Father has prepared a special place for us to sit in His kingdom. The aisle has been adorned with beautiful flowers, and at the end of the aisle is a man. He is a man full of the splendor of love. You are your beloved's, and His desire is for you (Song of Solomon 7:10). The Father is overjoyed to present us to His son, Jesus, your Prince and Heavenly Bridegroom. We are the Bride of Christ. We are the ones He came for, and we are the ones He will return for. When my heart was melted by this revelation, a few years after my abortion, suddenly my life had meaning again. I could believe again that I was someone special, someone worth fighting for.

Millions of women and families have experienced the emotional trauma that follows an abortion. Many of these women are walking around whole and healthy in appearance, but they still feel the pain of their trauma.

Several years after my abortion, this pain came to the surface in my life. At the time, I was convinced that I had moved on and was healed from all the pain. I had completed a post-abortion Bible study. I was sharing my testimony publicly, and I was ministering to women, helping them choose life for their babies. Yet in one moment, pain gripped me and slowly took over once again. I was working in a pregnancy center and serving a young lady who was choosing adoption for her growing baby. We sat down to chat about the adoption process and how she was handling it. Toward the end of our conversation, we began to watch a video that shared practical information about the next step in her process. As we watched the video that was meant to give her peace about her choice, extreme regret and sorrow flooded my soul. This sorrow had been buried by my declaration of my healing, but it was still deeply rooted in my soul. I was shocked by this, because I had gone through all the practical, suggested steps to healing. Surely, I was healed. So I had thought. But I was wrong.

Jesus knew what I needed. I needed more of Him. I needed to know Him in a real and more intimate way. I needed to feel what it felt like to be bought back and paid for once and for all. I wanted to rest in the warmth of His fiery love and passionate pursuit. I wanted to feel like a princess again, pursued by the King of Kings. These revelations of Him set me free. I became a new creation in Christ, and now, as I minister to other women, I realize that I have nothing to truly offer them outside of Jesus. He is their only answer. He is the solution. It is humbling to come to a place in our ministry where we realize that we truly have nothing to offer but Him. Our efforts are often important and necessary, but we have to remember who we are representing. We are only His hands and feet; He is the One who can bring true healing: spiritually, emotionally, and physically.

It is easy to get wrapped up in a cause or a social justice movement and forget about the One who brings true peace and reconciliation. He died, but He also rose again. He lives in us and has extended an invitation to us to live a supernatural and holy lifestyle, beyond simply overcoming trials and regrets. His invitation is an invitation to know Him intimately, in ways that will change our lives forever. We can all get to know Jesus more intimately. Spending time in worship, reading and mediating on the Word of God, joining a community of believers, and learning to hear the voice of God are all ways that we can dive deeper into the heart of God.

These simple yet practical disciplines are important to teach and model to the women and men whom God brings to us. We can equip and teach others how to posture themselves to know God. This starts with intentionality and discipline. When we sustain truth in our hearts and minds, true breakthrough will come. You can partner with God in a moment of deliverance or breakthrough for someone else, but they must learn how to walk with God and seek Him on their own. Even after receiving a miraculous healing, the hardest part of the journey can be putting one foot in front of the other and stepping out through our front door. The thoughts that decorated our past are still there. The chance of being rejected or accepted remains. When we have been keeping a terrible secret for so long and finally reveal it, it can be difficult to wade through the waters of our new life. Sustaining truth in our inner man through worship, the Word, and community, is required for true and lasting breakthrough. But having lived out these truths, I can now look back on that sixteen-year-old girl I used to be and barely recognize her. This is the power of the gospel and the ministry of Christ. The post-abortive women sitting in our church pews can walk arm in arm with their Judge, their Prince, and their Bridegroom, and finally find their home.

Chapter Nine

TESTIMONIES: OUR VOICE

When Jesus went ashore, He saw a large crowd, and He felt compassion for them
because they were like sheep without a shepherd;
and He began to teach them many things.

Mark 6:34

I HAVE MET SOME OF the bravest and most tenacious women in America. Their courageous words have filled the halls of courthouses, churches, conferences, and retreat centers across our country. With persistence and faith, their testimonies have come before lower courts, the Supreme Court, and the Court of Heaven. Even as I write this chapter, testimonies of over 3,000 women are reaching the ears of the Supreme Court justices in the case of *Whole Women's Health v. Hellerstedt*. These women have a powerful voice. They carry a powerful and sweeping authority to pray for justice in the courts, for healing for other women, for babies in the womb, and for the destiny of our nation. God is raising up an army of post-abortive women to decree, "Life!" These women keep coming. They keep speaking, and their numbers are growing. Joining them are former abortion workers, abortion doctors, and men who paid for abortions. From out of the rubble of their lives, from behind closed doors, many women are speaking. Their words are beginning to echo across our land.

Jesus is rescuing those who have fallen in the battle. He is redeeming time that has been stolen, memories that have been scarred, and lives that seemed doomed to tragedy and heartbreak. They are not only forgiven, but they are brought near the Father. In His lap, their breakthrough is assured and a new history with Him begins to unfold. Memories fill my mind of standing with women at the memorial services for their babies taken by abortion, of standing with them in front of abortion clinics, and of sharing our stories in churches and retreats. These are memorial stones in their lives and in their fight for life. Their path to breakthrough has not been easy, and their stories cannot be refuted or ignored.

In the midst of the chaotic sounds of the pro-choice gongs, I believe that healed post-abortive women and children saved from abortion are the key to the Church finding her voice. If we allow the words of these women and children to pierce the clouds of passivity, propaganda, and apathy surrounding the abortion issue, then all our voices will be soaked in compassion, understanding, and truth. Jesus is looking down at the crowds of women across our nation and our world who are like sheep without a

> God is raising up an army of post-abortive women to decree, "Life!" Joining them are former abortion workers, abortion doctors, and men who paid for abortions.

shepherd, and He is instructing them in His truth (Mark 6:34). We need to hear and heed their stories.

The remainder of this chapter is filled with stories of women who have found their breakthrough. They have either walked through an abortion, have been saved from an abortion, or walked away from an abortion. These women have affected my life and their stories have been woven into my own journey; I am honored to share them with you. I pray that their stories will also bring courage to women you know and will help them share their stories with someone else in need.

CHRISTINA BENNETT

My mother's 'Yes' saved my life. Over a decade ago, I stood in the bathroom of my parents' house while my mother struggled to find the words to speak. "You'll hate me," she said. "I can't tell you, because you'll hate me." "I would never hate you," I replied. The scared look in her eyes revealed that she wasn't convinced. I was in my early twenties, home for a visit from college, and engaged with her in a simple discussion that had suddenly become extremely serious. My mother wanted to tell me something important, but fear held her back. After reassuring her that I could handle whatever she had to say, she told me. She shared a secret that she had kept carefully hidden from me all my life. With great trepidation, she revealed to me that I had had an appointment to die.

It was 1980, before I was born. Her pregnancy test came back positive, so my mother, Andrea, now faced the sobering reality of being unmarried and with a child. Her boyfriend wasn't thrilled to hear the news, and abortion was highly recommended—pressured, in fact. She sought advice from her spiritual mentor, hoping to find solace in this mentor's often compassionate words. Comfort quickly eluded her, though, as her mentor, shockingly, said, "If you ever come back to this church, I will be the first person to put my foot in the door and not let you in."

So, uncertain of her future and lacking support, my mother made the awful appointment to abort me. She drove to Mount Sinai Hospital in Hartford, Connecticut, alone.

When she arrived, the staff gave her a cotton gown to change into. A counselor was assigned to meet with her before the procedure. After spilling out the circumstances, the counselor reassured her, saying, "You're making the best choice." But those soothing words spoken into Andrea's ears wrestled with an unpleasant knot in her stomach. She left the counselor's office and sat in a hallway near the waiting room. Andrea covered her face with her hands while tears trickled down her cheeks. As she quietly wept, an older woman—an African-American janitor—walked toward her, carrying a mop and pail. This stranger came close, lifted my mother's chin in her hand, and looked straight into her eyes.

"Do you want to have this baby?" she calmly asked.

Put at peace by the kindness of this stranger, Andrea answered "Yes."

"Then God will give you the strength," the woman said. "Put on your clothes and leave."

Moments later, the doctor called her name, and Andrea walked into the operating room. A gruesome sight awaited her on the floor: a puddle of blood left over from the last abortion. Gasping with disgust, she confessed that she had changed her mind. "No," the doctor said forcefully, "you're just nervous. You've already paid for this. Don't leave this room." The look in the doctor's eyes made Andrea suspect that he feared losing business—both hers and that of the women in the waiting room who would see her leave. He showed his anger as he argued with her to stay. In spite of his emotional pleas, Andrea confidently declared, "I'm leaving. I've changed my mind."

That was thirty-three years ago.

My mother's courageous decision to leave the hospital saved my life. To this day, my mother believes that the janitor in the hospital hallway was an angel from heaven. She says that the woman's eyes were like pools of water. Whether she was an angel or a human, I will probably never know while on this earth. What I do know is that I had an appointment to die . . . but God canceled that appointment. Instead, I received the priceless gift of life—a gift for which I am forever grateful. Thank you, Mom, for saying "yes" to me and letting me live.

Today, Christina serves as the Client Services Manager at the ABC Women's Center, a Care-Net-affiliated pregnancy resource center, where she counsels women who are considering an abortion. In addition, she is a writer for Live Action News, Bound4Life, and at her personal blog, www.chrismarie.com. Christina is a speaker for the National Black Pro-Life Coalition, and she works to raise up voices to end abortion in the Black community. She is a wife, stepmother, and a licensed Christian minister.

JOANNE FECI

When I was little, I wanted to be a missionary. I wanted to be a nun so I could devote my life to God. I wanted to be an obstetrician so I could deliver babies. I also wanted to be a mother and a wife. But when I was fifteen, all those dreams were stolen from me; or so I thought. As I sit and think about the darkest, most difficult time in my life, I cannot help but to rejoice in all that has been birthed from it.

When I was fifteen years old I found out that I was pregnant. I was forced to abort my baby at 16.5 weeks gestation. To describe that day as a horror movie would be an understatement. It took counseling and a miracle to get me back on my feet physically, emotionally, and spiritually—only for me to be raped by my baby's father and become pregnant again the following year. Once again I was forced to abort my child. I was numb, broken, confused, scared, and ashamed beyond reason. I lost every drop of self-respect I had. I turned to drugs, smoking, drinking, and sleeping around, in a futile attempt to numb the pain. I felt that I deserved to die. So I didn't graduate from college, or become a doctor, or even become a useful member of society. Instead, I hung out with strippers and drug dealers and people who had no ambition in life.

Thankfully, God had a different plan for me.

Several years later I began dating a guy, and while we were dating he came to know Jesus. He soon began traveling the world as a missionary, doing things I had always dreamt of doing. I was jealous. So one night at work I prayed and asked God if He were real, and if so, to please prove it to me. I was convinced that if He could redeem my alcoholic boyfriend, surely He could do something for me. I knew that with the way I was living I would either end up in jail, pregnant again, with an STD . . . or dead. The following day I received a letter from Mexico, from my boyfriend. In the letter, he spoke things to my heart that made me realize that the letter was the answer to my prayer of the night before. I gave my life to the Lord that very night.

Little by little, God began to transform and change my heart and mind. As my hunger for Him grew, so did my faith. Not only faith in Him, but faith in what He can do with a broken past. He began to show me what He saw in me and how He felt about me. I realized that no matter how badly I thought I had ruined my life, there was still hope. Not only hope to get by, but even hope for my fairy tale and true redemption of all the things I had lost.

In the years since then, God has given me every dream of my heart: all the dreams I felt I did not deserve as a post-abortive, broken young woman. God helped me believe for my dreams. I began to pursue my dreams to travel the world as a missionary, and I ended up living for several years in England as a missionary and youth worker, as well as traveling to Italy and Scotland. Though after my abortion I did not believe I deserved to get married, in 2004 I met the love of my life, a man of great love, strength, and character. Above all of my dreams, I certainly did not believe that I deserved children. God thought differently, though, and He gave me two beautiful boys. They are my gifts from God.

The Lord has used my story to help others along the way, but, even more importantly, to show me and those around me the power of mercy, redemption, and grace. Through the birth of my sons, my love of life and pregnancy and birth were all reignited. I became a doula, a labor coach, and am now just three years away from becoming a nurse-midwife. The road has been long, and it has not been easy. Even after becoming a Christian, it took years to heal from the death of my first two babies, but when I look back I can see that all my little-girl dreams have been redeemed.

Yes, I still grieve the children whom I lost, but not as often as before. I do think of how old they would be today and wonder what they would be like if they were here. However, my heart is also filled with joy and gratitude that God did not leave me where I was. He took me from the depths of darkness and filled me with His light.

NATASHA EDWARDS

In September of 2009 I was in my freshmen year of college at Texas Tech in Waco, Texas. For an entire week it was very difficult to make it to my morning classes, as I was terribly nauseated. I decided to take a pregnancy test, and the positive result glared back at me. As I shared the news with my boyfriend, we both became excited, yet we were also scared and confused. I was a 19-year-old girl full of ambition, and I wondered how a baby could fit into my life.

At first, my boyfriend proposed that we get married and plan for the arrival of our baby. But within one week, everything changed. The possibility of marriage and having a child together vanished. My heart sank as I realized that my future with my boyfriend was over. He was gone, leaving me with $250 to pay for an abortion. He had decided that he wanted neither our child nor me; we would only get in the way of his life dreams and ambitions. I did want my baby, yet I could understand my boyfriend's desire to move on. There was a part of me that wanted to move on as well. For about two weeks, I kept my pregnancy a secret. I cried a lot, but finally I broke down; I had to tell someone. I told a friend of my family who lived nearby.

I confided in this family friend and asked her advice about having an abortion. She was very much against it. She was a strong Christian and she immediately began to pray with me. She even tried to reach out to my ex-boyfriend, but without success. She tried to convince me not to have the abortion, but she actually drove me all the way to Austin, Texas, to my abortion appointment, about one month later. She was reluctant to take me, but she wanted me to have someone with me as I proceeded rather than have me go alone. She stayed in the car when we arrived: praying that I would change my mind.

I was scared and numb as I walked into the clinic and began filling out the paperwork. Soon the staff directed me to a video I was required to watch before they could proceed with the abortion. As I started to watch the video, I knew that I had to leave. Suddenly, I jumped up from my chair and ran out the door as fast as I could. I left so fast that I forgot my ID card and so, unfortunately, I had to go back in. My spirit was so disturbed as I sat inside that clinic that I could not go through with the abortion. I know now that there were angels in that room, and the prayers of my friend sitting in the parking lot were moving my heart. I ran outside to my friend, and she went back into the clinic with me to tell them that I would not be having an abortion that day.

Today I have a fifteen-year-old son named Elijah. He is the joy of my heart. He is creative, smart, full of life, and has great dreams for his life. I am a proud mother, and I know that running out of that clinic was the best choice I have ever made. Not only do I get to live life with my son, but also everything else that my heart desired to do in life is being accomplished. I earned my bachelor's degree in Business Administration, I've been serving as an intercessory missionary for eight years at the International House of Prayer in Atlanta, and I have traveled to a number of countries on mission trips. God is still fulfilling all His promises to me and my son. I am so thankful that, together, we have hope and a great future.

JULIE THOMAS

March 6th, 1978, was the day that my life changed forever.

I was raised a Christian in a loving home, and I had been dating my boyfriend for four years. We had made a promise to each other early in our relationship that we would not have sex until we were married. But, at the age of eighteen, I initiated sex with him and, six months later, I became pregnant. My boyfriend wanted to get married and have our baby. That was all I had ever really wanted as a young girl, to be a wife and a mother. But for reasons that I don't even remember now, I became frightened and decided to exercise my right to "choose."

Now I know that I was choosing to take part in killing my pre-born baby. My parents did not even know I was pregnant and my boyfriend would never have agreed with me to abort our child, so I didn't tell him. While at the abortion facility, I received counseling that "it wasn't a baby yet," just a "clump of cells" or "tissue." They told me whatever I needed to hear to go through with the abortion. I was also given an ultrasound, but I wasn't allowed to see the picture. (I had no idea what an ultrasound even was.) I was then informed that I was too far along in my pregnancy to have an easy abortion, that I would have to stay overnight for a two-day procedure and it would cost more. I then became fearful and decided to leave and tell my parents that I was getting married and having a baby. But some of the staff followed me outside to my car and told me that they had made a mistake. They said, "Come back inside, we'll take care of the problem, and you will never think about this day again."

I know now that the "problem" was actually a developing pre-born baby, my baby. But I believed their lie, followed them back inside, and proceeded to have my baby torn apart and ripped from the safest place that a baby can be. After bleeding for three weeks, I finally had to be hospitalized and have surgery performed by my mother's doctor: the same doctor who had delivered me, eighteen years earlier. I almost died, as I had had an incomplete abortion. You see, my baby had indeed been too large (she was probably eighteen or nineteen weeks old) for me to have a simple abortion, and pieces of my baby had been left inside me. I had then developed an infection: an infection that even today women still die from. God was certainly with me that day (as well as every day), as the doctor thought that I would also have to have a hysterectomy, and that would have prevented me from ever having other children. That was too much for my eighteen-year-old mind to process.

In the next twenty-three years, I had two more children and a miscarriage (which made me think I was being punished), divorced three husbands, had relationship problems, experienced many unhealthy relationships with the wrong men, was obsessed with becoming pregnant again (a replacement baby), suffered from unending depression, anxiety attacks, tremendous guilt, shame, sadness, and psychological "numbing," and abused alcohol and drugs. I also suffered from emotional numbness, over-protectiveness of my children when they were young, and I greatly missed my aborted child.

Finally, in 2000, at the age of forty-one, a friend of mine told me about an abortion that she had had when she was in college. I immediately began to tell her my story, and right then, my healing began. God soon directed me to a Bible study for post-abortive women, and since 2001 I have been a part of Operation Outcry, an international group of women and men who speak out on how we have suffered due to our abortions. I have served on an advisory committee for Operation Outcry, have become politically involved, volunteer at my local pregnancy center, and lead a post-abortive Bible study. In 2004 I also became an international pro-life missionary.

God has blessed me with opportunities that I never would have imagined. I've been given the opportunity to speak with young adults in schools and colleges, medical schools, churches, and youth groups. I've also given my testimony in churches, at pro-life fundraisers, to government legislators, and on television and radio shows. I even had a private meeting with the Catholic Archbishop of Quito, Ecuador. God has taken my pain and truly turned it into my passion and His glory.

TIFFANY FLOCK

In Proverbs 31, the mother of King Lemuel is handing down some wisdom to her son. She begins by saying "What shall I say to you, my son? What wisdom can I impart, child of my womb?" She continues, "Speak out on behalf of those who have no voice, and defend all those who have been passed over" (The Voice Translation).

Why are these Scriptures so important to my testimony? Because when I was fifteen years old, I found out that I was pregnant. As soon as my mother told my father, he decided

I was too young, and that I would be aborting the child in my womb. Neither my dad nor my mom were ever told that abortion was murder, not by their parents nor by anyone in the church.

I once heard someone say that "one generation's compromise leads to another generation's bondage." I see that truth active in my family line. My parents drove me to the abortion clinic. Outside, it was a beautiful, sunny day, but inside, it was scary. There were so many young girls waiting their turn. After the abortion, I got in the car with my parents . . . and screamed from the pain. We drove away, and did not discuss the issue again until I was in my twenties. Sadly, I ended up getting pregnant and aborting two more children before I was twenty years old. The door of death was open in my life.

After my second abortion, at seventeen years old, I was rushed to the hospital. We discovered that the doctor had left my baby's arms and legs inside me, and I had to be hospitalized to remove them. Several years later, I went to the abortion clinic yet again. This time the doctor only gave me pain medication and then ripped the baby from my womb as I lay there, screaming. The doctor looked at me and, in a stern voice, told me to be quiet so the other girls couldn't hear me. From that point on, I never discussed what I had gone through with anyone. I had no voice.

What that doctor spoke over me made me silent for years. Yet one fateful day, God in His mercy came down and touched me with wisdom and revelation about what I had done. After months of healing my broken heart, God revealed to me the meaning of Proverbs 31. I was then able to forgive my parents, their parents, the church, and myself for not being a voice for the voiceless. He faithfully took away all my shame and opened my lips. The seal the doctor put on my mouth that day was removed. Now I am a voice for the voiceless, and my husband and I are raising two beautiful girls to do the same. The time to speak out is now.

PATTI GIEBINK

I first met Cathy Harris in January 2007 at the house of Matt and Kim Lockett, who work with Bound4Life International. We were all attending the Call Relaunch in Fort Mill, South Carolina, in preparation for the upcoming Call Nashville event that July. The Call brings together thousands of Christians in stadiums to worship, pray, and fast for revival and massive change in America, and we were each scheduled to participate in the event.

There we were, my dear friend Amy Hofer and I, sitting on the floor talking in Matt and Kim's living room with Cathy and another friend and leader, Liz Robertson. During the conversation, Amy relentlessly continued to nudge me, saying "tell them; . . . tell them." It's not easy, in a room full of women harmed by abortion, to casually mention that I had been an abortion doctor for Planned Parenthood. That's not a great conversation icebreaker. Finally, I found the courage and blurted out the truth of my past. Cathy and Liz were visibly shocked, yet we were able to talk through the discomfort. That conversation, the shock on their faces, and the discomfort I felt in the room have been repeated multiple times in the presence of other pro-lifers. Some of the conversations have ended well, but others have not.

The night before The Call Nashville arrived, and I found myself in a meeting with the other participants, awaiting our instructions. Lou Engle, the founder of The Call, asked out loud if I was there. He had asked me to represent abortion providers for "identification/representative repentance" during a segment to be focused on praying for the ending of abortion. Sheepishly, I raised my hand, although I wanted to crawl under my chair and hide. I felt the shock in the room all over again as my hand went up in the air.

The next day, July 7, 2007, with over 70,000 pro-life people in the Tennessee Titans' stadium and 2.5 million more watching worldwide on GodTV, we gathered. I waited in the green room until I was called to go to the pre-stage area. Soon, I made my way alone to the little stage just below the main stage. Then it was my turn to join Lou Engle on stage. Cathy was already there, with her pastor and several other women; they were praying for her. I sat down, watching and feeling so very alone, but not yet feeling the full weight of being the "enemy."

Finally, we were called to the main stage. Cathy gave her testimony first, as Will Ford and I stood behind her. As she spoke, repenting for women who have had abortions, her words pierced my heart, and I couldn't help but drop to my knees. The weight of all the innocent lives murdered through abortion fell on my shoulders and pushed my face into the ground. My eyeglasses scattered and I cried, pleading: "Lord, I can't do this!" Still sobbing uncontrollably (and I rarely ever cry), I felt Lou Engle lifting me up, then, without any introduction, he handed me the microphone. Through my sobs, I stammered out, "I'm Patti; . . . Dr. Patti." More sobbing came, until I heard someone in front of the stage yell, "We love you, Patti!" Others began to join in. Encouragement filled my heart, and I was able to repent for myself and all the other abortion doctors whose hands had shed innocent blood (Proverbs 6:17). I then managed to recite the Bound4Life creed: "Jesus, I plead your blood over my sins and the sins of my nation. God, end abortion and send revival to America."

I finished sharing and stepped to the back, still sobbing, when another national leader came close to me. She hugged me and whispered to me, "For all the mothers and grandmothers who will never hold their children and grandchildren . . . we forgive you." In that moment I felt all the guilt and shame lift from me, and truly my face changed! It was like a face transplant, as God healed me from all the guilt and condemnation I had been carrying. Once and for all, Jesus took my sin and replaced it with everlasting peace and forgiveness. Hallelujah, praise the Lord! His mercy endures forever.

Chapter Ten

BOUND FOR LIFE

"I am the Way, the Truth, and the Life."

John 14:6

FROM THE DIRKSEN SENATE OFFICE building, I walked up to the United States Supreme Court, until my toes kissed the first step. I stood gazing up at the impenetrable bronze doors. Looking foolish with a piece of red tape covering my mouth and the word "Life" written on it, I prayed a silent, faith-filled prayer, the Bound4Life-band prayer: "Jesus, I plead your blood over my sins and the sins of my nation. God, end abortion and bring revival to America." As I prayed, I remembered that angry teenage girl I had been. I was sad for her, as if she never had been me. That young woman was gone. She had faced her Goliath, the abortion industry, and had fallen prey to it. She had lost that battle and was left in devastation and tears, and without her child. I closed my eyes as I stood next to dear friends. I could hear the pro-abortion mockers and antagonists behind us, but they were fading in the background. "It's a woman's right," they chanted. The mocking continued, but my faith increased. I faced the giant again.

This time, in my spirit, in God, I found a place of solitude, peace, and confidence. The red tape covering my lips seeped purpose into every fiber of my being.

I have prayed this faith-filled prayer hundreds, if not thousands, of times since the first time I prayed in front of the Supreme Court. I have prayed with that red piece of tape on my mouth at the steps of the Supreme Court, at the steps of lower courts across the nation, and in front of abortion clinics. Sometimes I feel like David standing in front of Goliath, with God on my side. But whether I'm standing in front of the Supreme Court or in the court of Heaven from inside my prayer room, I know there is victory. Even though I still hear my accuser remind me (just as he did the first day I prayed this audacious prayer) that I am just a small, insignificant, stay-at-home mom. Who am I to believe that God will hear my prayers and will move mountains on my behalf? I hear the antagonists and I run, full-speed, to my Heavenly Father. But I do believe. I do believe that God hears my prayers and the prayers of hundreds of other women, asking Him to spare another woman and her baby from the devastation we have been through. I do believe that abortion will end because of the prayers of the saints. I have to believe it, because I have to have hope for America.

The Goliath of the abortion industry will not step aside easily. I am not naïve enough to believe that all abortion will cease at the sound of the gavel's judgment. Even if abortion is made illegal, it is possible that abortions will continue illegally through stronger forms of "birth control" and "forced miscarriages." Nevertheless, I pray that one day our nation will break its agreement with the evil Goliath of abortion, and as a result millions of babies, women, men, and families will be saved. Women will be heard, we will hold our children in our arms, and the church will be called from the outfield up to bat.

God is already on the move. Despite the façade presented by the media and some political establishments, the abortion industry is weakening. We can see it crumbling. Through the ministry of Bound4Life International, thousands of believers all across our nation and internationally are praying for the end of abortion. Bound4Life is mobilizing the Church to step up to bat, with red "life tape" over our mouths, in front of our state capitols and neighborhood abortion clinics to silently pray. Along with Bound4Life, other ministries, such as 40 Days for Life, are also exponentially growing in numbers in front of abortion clinics and seeing miraculous results. Babies are being saved, abortion clinics are closing at rapid rates, workers are leaving the industry and exposing the deception inside their walls, videos showing hellish practices within the abortion clinics have gone viral, pro-life legislation is being passed by more and more states, and popular opinion is swaying towards life. This is thrilling. A great move of God is on the horizon, and He is calling our name to come with Him.

The tide is turning, and I believe it is in direct conjunction with the Church returning to God in prayer and repentance. We are called to usher His kingdom onto the earth and to be His hands and feet. He does not need us, yet He has asked us to partner with Him in prayer and in deed. This is the way God has transformed nations throughout history. Revivals and major cultural change have always started with the Church's prayers and repentance (or the lack of it). When I was working in college ministry I spent several months studying the

Hebrides Revival in Scotland, which took place in the late 1940s to early 1950s. I was able to lead a trip to the islands in order to pray and sit with brothers and sisters in the faith who had experienced that revival. I was overwhelmed as they recounted the stories of hundreds of people in the villages suddenly filling the churches and fields to worship God. These small islands off the coast of Scotland experienced a move of God like they had never seen, and it all began with two simple women: two desperate, 80-year-old women crying out to God in the midst of spiritual drought and crisis. And the Hebrides Revival is only one example of many revivals that have begun in a home or a church where a few desperate saints were crying out to God on behalf of their land. Second Chronicles 7:14 states, "if my people who are called by My name humble themselves, and pray and seek My face and turn from their wicked ways, then I will hear from heaven, will forgive their sin, and will heal their land." God has fulfilled His promise time and time again. He will never fail to keep His promises, but we must do our part.

There are times when God allows us to see a nation's or an individual's potential, despite their present circumstances. God shares this future information with us so that we can agree with Him for their destiny to grow to fruition. You may have already experienced God's leading to pray in this way for someone in your family, your church, your neighborhood, or for your nation. Praying for the end of abortion is one way that we can join with Him to see America's divine destiny come to pass.

Even when judgment is prepared in Heaven for Earth, God still listens when we pray. God was ready to judge the Israelites for worshipping idols and forgetting that it was He who had delivered them

(Exodus 32:7), but Moses stood in the gap and reminded God of His mercy and love for the Israelites (Exodus 32:9–13). The Scripture tells us that Moses literally changed God's mind (Exodus 32:14). His prayers and intercession changed the present and future for the nation of Israel. This is true intercession; Moses contended in the court of Heaven until he saw results. We deserve judgment for the horrible national sin of abortion. Yet, in His mercy, God is calling for intercessors to cry out for mercy just as Moses did for Israel.

The Scripture says that God looks for "a man who will build a wall and stand in the gap" on behalf of the land (Ezekiel 22:30). Standing in the gap, building a wall with your own body in prayer, is not glamorous, yet it is one of the most effective ways to see true results in our nation. It is in this place of humility right up next to the Lord's heart that we can hear His purposes, they can become our own, and we can pray those purposes into reality. We gain clarity, cease from striving, and are compelled to act as God leads.

We cannot use our present circumstances or busyness as an excuse for not partnering with God in the way He leads.

Many of us will be called to remain in this place of prayer and seize the everyday opportunities that God puts in front of us. Others will be called to lay down their personal ambitions and plans in order to care for an orphan who needs a family or a young girl who needs practical help to choose life for her baby. And these callings can change as our lives change. My efforts are much different now than they were as a single woman. I am now a mother to three beautiful children, and many of those more "glamorous" days of public action have passed, at least for the present. I still have opportunities to practically help and speak on abortion, yet most of my days are spent caring for and homeschooling my three children. I wake up with them in the night when their tummy hurts or when they have a bad dream. My prayer time mostly happens in my office in the wee hours of the morning or while I am washing dishes. The practical ways in which I partner with God have shifted, though my heart's desire to partner with Him has not. My season has changed as my life circumstances have changed, and so will yours. But we cannot use our present circumstances or busyness as an excuse for not partnering with God in the way He leads. There are practical ways for all us to help if we are willing.

Because I responded years ago to God's call to be a voice for women and children, I still expect the opportunities, whether through organized ministry or at the grocery store. Because I have asked Him to, God sends across my path pregnant girls who need assistance and an encouraging word to take the next step into parenting. Someone very close to me experienced an unexpected pregnancy, and I helped her choose adoption for her baby. I have walked with her this past year through the grieving process of a birth mother who must separate from her baby. God has also called me to share my story with women in mom's groups and homeschool groups. The "yes" in my spirit has not faded.

All around us, people are hurting. We don't have to have an organized ministry in order to help them. We simply have to live out a culture of life. You may be called to start a ministry and if so, that is wonderful. No matter what you do, though, when you take hold of God's heart for the unborn and their mothers, He will give you opportunities to be a voice for them. He is faithful to lead anyone who is willing to follow.

I dare you: ask God to direct your path. Give yourself to praying for an individual whom God brings into your life, for the pregnancy center in your neighborhood, for governmental leaders, for abortion workers, and for our nation as a whole. In those times when you don't know what to pray, say "Jesus, I plead your blood over my sins and the sins of my nation. God, end abortion and send revival to America." Every time you pray this prayer, you will be joining in a continuing prayer meeting alongside thousands of other believers around the world. Partnering with God is not about striving, but about resting in the ebbs and flows of the journey. By partnering with God, you can sometimes move mountains in seconds that would have taken years of your own strength and efforts to move. I do know this: when the intentional steps of our feet and the prayerful words of our mouths marry, we will most certainly see miracles.

Listen to the words of Dietrich Bonhoeffer, a faithful Christian in the midst of the terrible, and terrifying, Nazi regime. "To be silent does not mean to be inactive; rather it means to breathe in the will of God, to listen attentively and be ready to obey." Bonhoeffer was not referring to a neglectful or careless silence, but a prayerful and obedient stance before God. Be silent in prayer, and then go where God sends you with His strategies from Heaven. We need to walk in God's plans. His plans can use the faith of a mustard seed generated in the place of prayer to change the face of a community or the direction of an entire nation. He has great blueprints to give you, your family, and your church community to put His love in action.

Let us put our love—and God's—into action, and ask Him to transform our communities. Let us not be scared of messes, sacrifice, or difficulties. Will you join me in my dream to see abortion-free communities across our nation? I long to see communities where the womb is a safe place again and where women are truly cared for. This is the gospel. This is a culture of life. Don't be afraid to start small. It is far better to have a continual and sustainable "yes" in our lives than it is to try to go big and burn out. Many small efforts of love and honor in a community soon come together to create a whole. The whole communicates that you care. The whole, over a period of time, creates a culture and a way of life. A consistent "yes" communicates to the community around us not only that we care but that we are not afraid. We are not afraid of our church filling up with babies. We are not afraid of bringing people into our homes. We are not afraid of imperfection.

I am amazed by the communities I have walked arm-in-arm with through the years. God has released vision and faith that is remarkable, simple, and life-changing, because He has people willing to act. Here are just a few practical ways in which fellow Christians are serving others. Church communities are starting pregnancy centers inside their church buildings, staffing it with volunteer church members, and funding the practical needs of women and babies. Churches are adopting neighborhood pregnancy centers, providing volunteers, funds, and even baby showers for women who choose life for their babies. I was a part of a community that started an adoption agency within the community, in order for their own members and others to adopt children at a fraction of the cost other private agencies charge. Christian families are providing homes for women until their baby is born and both mother and child are in a stable permanent environment. I have friends who have adopted children at risk of being aborted, or fostered children in need of a safe environment.

Communities are hosting "date nights" for foster and adoptive parents, so they can have a night out to be refreshed. Churches and foundations are funding adoptions. Sidewalk counselors are in front of abortion clinics offering to adopt or direct a woman to a place she can get practical help. Abortion recovery groups are found in churches all across the nation. Communities are helping abortion workers financially, in order to help them get out of the industry. The opportunities are endless. There are any number of large and small ways by which we can all make a huge difference in the lives of children, women, and families.

Christians should set the standard for the rest of the nation. Our nation is watching us. Our nation needs to know what the Church thinks about abortion, and how we will respond in the next few years as the truth about abortion continues to come to the forefront of the public stage.

Simply stating that we are opposed to abortion is not enough to bring about change. Are our Christian communities front and center, instructing our nation in truth, or are we hanging out in the outfield allowing the truth to be lost or misrepresented? Are we jumping in to help and disciple those who are hurting and coming into the Kingdom, or are we merely counting up our salvation cards in the back room? Many times we celebrate that a girl decides to cancel an abortion appointment, but then what help will she have? What kind of life will the child have? Does the mother know her options for adoption? Planned Parenthood has made their "help" openly known and readily available. Convincing a woman not to get an abortion without our being willing to help her is like leading someone in a salvation prayer yet never directing them to a church home or instructing them in the faith. We can stand up in church and state proudly that 100 people got saved during our outreach or ten babies were saved at the abortion clinic, but what happens to these people when they get home and the devil pounds them over the head with his lies about their situation? Where will they turn? Yes, God moves, convicts, and saves lives in a single moment, but we have to be willing to be there for that woman and her baby when she needs our help.

The generation of young people who are in the womb today are called to greatness; these young people are worth the effort to rescue them. The enemy has engaged in an all-out assault on the womb because of this generation's God-ordained destiny. We must have eyes to see the battle, face it head on, and engage in it with sacrificial love.

But I have to ask myself: what will happen when abortion ends? How does my prayer of faith actually impact my life? Am I willing to be the answer to my own prayer? There are already hundreds of children living in the foster care system or orphanages who have been given the chance of life. There will be a flood of babies added to the number of children waiting for a forever family if abortion on demand is no longer an option for women. There are already women who choose abortion because they fear for their child's future. Of course this is no reason to choose death, but it is a very real and understandable concern.

We need good mothers and fathers who will stand up for these women and children. We need entire church communities who will be willing to adopt. This is not only how the church ends abortion, but the only answer if and when it ends. Some of us working in the pro-life arena might have to switch gears if the abortion industry collapses. The primary purpose of our organizations might go from fighting to end abortion to providing homes for children and women in need who would have chosen abortion. Are we willing to lose our pro-life jobs, to make the switch in ministry, and even to put our comfortable lifestyles on the altar? These are very real possibilities in the coming days if God answers our prayers.

Sometimes I wonder what life would be like if I had not aborted my baby. I wonder if I would have found the community and support I needed. Would I have been looked at as a failure? Would my baby and I have been fully adopted into our community? How would that have impacted my future marriage and family? Questions, wonderings, and remembrance will always remain with me, as they remain with every other post-abortive woman. When I see beautiful pre-teen girls, I often think of Hannah and the age she would be now. Every year on October 13th, the anniversary of my abortion, I remember her.

For many years, the events of that day flashed before my eyes like a nightmare that would not stop pursuing me. I will never forget that day, but now I have come to expect the sweet presence of the Lord during my reminiscing. It now represents a day to honor my daughter and the sweet journey I have been on with Jesus. I have built new memories, laid down new memorial stones, and found my voice in the midst of all the noise of the pro-choice and the pro-life movements. This is the life available to all post-abortive women.

Sharing my story, helping women, and supporting the unborn has become one of the greatest honors in my life. Though I wish I could be holding my sweet Hannah in my arms, I am thankful that she has not been forgotten. Her life and purpose lives on in me and my family. In the few short weeks that she was alive, she impacted my life in ways I could have never imagined. Hannah is my hero. Because of her, I found Jesus.

About a year ago, I was sharing some of my stories with a local women's group. Many of the women in that room were my dear friends, but none of them knew my abortion and post-abortion story. The more I began to invest my life in these women, though, the more I realized that unless they knew my whole story they did not really know me. My abortion and post-abortion story has become a part of who I am and the call God has on my life. As I shared my story with these women, tears welled up in my eyes. Although I have shared my story countless times, I felt as if I were sharing it with family, and for the first time. It was fresh, raw, and real as I spoke while watching these moms rock and nurse their babies.

Although I have three other babies now, the loss of my first child never leaves me. I miss her. Many of the post-abortive women in America miss their babies as well. They daydream of rocking their baby to sleep. Without the hope and healing that God can give them, playgrounds bring only painful memories and baby showers bring the pain of what could have been. For ten years, twenty years, and sometimes even their entire lives, their eyes well with tears behind their sunglasses as they sit at the playground with their other children or grandchildren. Under their business suits and Friday night party dresses, their hearts ache. Dreams of their aborted children visit them after a long day of class, work, or ministry. Silenced due to lies, shame, or reputation, thousands of women live this way, never knowing that life can be different. I lived that way until Jesus changed my life.

There is a pair of double doors waiting for every one of those women to walk through. Maybe she already walks through them every Sunday morning, never knowing the freedom available to her on the other side. Maybe she's your neighbor, waiting for you to escort her through them. Maybe the woman who longs for that grand entrance is you. The doors may not be fancy. You might not like the shag carpet on the other side of them, but I assure you, the life found on the other side of your pain is worth it. Yes, the past will creep in from time to time, but Jesus is always ready to waltz with His daughter when she needs a healing dance with Him. He is the Prince of Peace. He is the Bridegroom King. Because of who He is, there is hope. There is hope for the mothers in our nation aching for another chance to hold their precious baby. There is hope for the babies God brings into the womb, waiting for their chance at life. There is hope for families and marriages that have been devastated by abortion. There is hope for America and the nations of the earth. Hope in Jesus never disappoints.

REFLECTIONS

MY LIFE IS NOT QUIET now, what with two more babies, home-schooling, and the everyday realities of marriage and family, but it is fulfilling. I don't view my past experiences as great successes, but simply as a demonstration of the mercy of God that is available to all of us, regardless of our mistakes. The years I spent in college ministry chasing after God, sitting in prayer rooms, joining faith-filled prayer meetings, and sharing my testimony on stages across the East Coast dug a deep well in my soul. They dug a well of intimacy and faith in God and hope for America. Though life doesn't look quite the same as it did before, I am still sharing the testimony that God began to build that day when I walked through those double doors of the Wesley Foundation. I've also had the opportunity to minister to couples every week as a childbirth and breastfeeding educator. Many times I don't know the journey that these couples are on, yet I get to touch a piece of their lives and experience the joy of welcoming their new baby into the world.

On my way home from teaching a childbirth class recently, I was pondering the excitement that I had just witnessed in six couples, over their first baby forming in the mother's womb. I thought about some of the conversations I had just been a part of, such as which crib and car seat to buy and when to have their first baby shower. These couples were overjoyed and delighted. They understood the truth of the development of their baby and the joy that it would be to be their child's parent. God gave each of them their baby to be a blessing, not a burden, just as He gives all of us babies to be blessings, regardless of the path they took to get to the womb.

As I continued driving that night, ready to see my own babies, I began to think about this book. Suddenly, a song came on the radio. The song, "You Are More," by Tenth Avenue North, is about a girl searching for answers in the midst of pain and loneliness and surrounded by her mistakes. In one of the verses, she says, "How did I get here? I'm not who I once was and I'm crippled by the fear that I've fallen too far to love." She then begins to have this love song sung over her, reminding her that her choices do not define her, but God Himself defines her. The song continues, "she is more than the choice that she's made, and more than the sum of her past mistakes."

As I listened, tears welled up in my eyes as I thought about all the women like me who have had abortions. I thought about the women who would be sitting in the pews of churches all across America that next Sunday, considering having an abortion. I thought about the women living with the shame of their abortion, trying to be strong on the outside so that you and I would never learn their secret. Those women need to hear this beautiful truth: that they are far more than the sum of their past mistakes. In the face of the terrible, but often abstract and impersonal, reality of abortion, they are real people who need real answers and real help. Jesus is asking us to help them: "As you did it for the least of these, you did it unto me."

For more information about

Cathy Harris

and

Created to Live
please visit:

www.cathyharris.org
@Cathy_Harris
Instagram: marycatharris
www.facebook.com/MaryCatHarris

For more information about
AMBASSADOR INTERNATIONAL
please visit:

www.ambassador-international.com
@AmbassadorIntl
www.facebook.com/AmbassadorIntl